Guidance and counselling in British schools

a discussion of current issues

edited by

Hugh Lytton and Maurice Craft

Edward Arnold (Publishers) Ltd

© Edward Arnold (Publishers) Ltd 1969

First published 1969

SBN: 7131 1565 3

Printed in Great Britain by
Western Printing Services Ltd Bristol

Contents

List of Contributors   4

Foreword   5

PART ONE: THE SOCIAL CONTEXT

1. Guidance, counselling and social needs *Maurice Craft*   9
   A Comment on Chapter One   *Robin Pedley*   24

PART TWO: THE COUNSELLOR AND THE SCHOOL

2. The School Counsellor from the Local Education
   Authority's viewpoint   *Raymond Gawthorpe*   29
3. The School Counsellor from
   the Headteacher's viewpoint—I   *A. W. Rowe*   35
4. The School Counsellor from
   the Headteacher's viewpoint—II   *Helen Whale*   44
   A Comment on Part Two   *Paul Kline*   48

PART THREE: THE COUNSELLOR AND OUTSIDE AGENCIES

5. The School Counsellor and
   the Child Guidance Clinic   *George Robb*   53
6. The School Counsellor and the
   Youth Employment Service   *Catherine Avent*   63
   A Comment on Part Three   *John Cowie*   71

PART FOUR: PERSPECTIVES ON COUNSELLING

7. An integrated approach to counselling and social
   work—a look into the future   *Hugh Lytton*   79
   A Comment on Chapter Seven   *R. Leslie Reid*   93
8. Some Practical Issues   *C. James Gill*   96
9. Postscript   *Hugh Lytton*   103

Bibliography   109

Index   111

Contributors

Catherine Avent, M.A., *Careers Guidance Adviser, Inner London Education Authority.*

John Cowie, M.B., Ch.B., D.P.M., M.P.S., *Medical Director, Roehampton and East Ham Child Psychiatric Clinics.*

Maurice Craft, B.Sc. (Econ.), *Senior Lecturer in Education, University of Exeter Institute of Education.*

Raymond Gawthorpe, B.A., *Assistant Education Officer, Hampshire County Council.*

C. James Gill, C.B., M.A., B.Sc., *Senior Lecturer in Education, University of Keele, Institute of Education.*

Paul Kline, B.A., M.Ed., Ph.D., *Lecturer in Education, University of Exeter Institute of Education.*

Hugh Lytton, M.A., Ph.D., *Lecturer in Education, Tutor-in-Charge, Educational Guidance and Counselling Course, University of Exeter Institute of Education.*

Robin Pedley, M.A., Ph.D., *Professor of Education, Director, University of Exeter Institute of Education.*

R. Leslie Reid, M.A., F.B.Ps.S., *Professor of Psychology, University of Exeter.*

George Robb, M.A., Ed.B., *Psychologist to the Education Committee, Essex County Council.*

A. W. Rowe, B.A., M.Phil., L.R.A.M., *Headmaster, David Lister Comprehensive School, Hull.*

Helen Whale, *Deputy Headmistress, Mayfield School, Inner London Education Authority.*

Foreword

A national conference on *Guidance and Counselling in British Schools* was held at Exeter University in July 1968. The conference was designed to examine, clarify and evaluate some of the most significant issues, theoretical and practical, relating to the appointment of counsellors in British schools which is now just beginning. The chapters of this book represent the edited papers and additional commentaries arising out of the conference, with the exception of Chapter 3 which is an adapted version of a paper that first appeared in *New Education*, February 1968.

Although the symposium reflects our conviction that the professionalisation of 'pastoral care' in British schools is necessary and desirable, it is intended to be *exploratory*, and not propagandist. The implications of this development both for the individual and for society are likely to be far-reaching, and this publication will have served its purpose if it provokes discussion as well as interest, and encourages careful and continuous evaluation.

HUGH LYTTON
MAURICE CRAFT

University of Exeter
October 1968

Acknowledgements

The Publisher's thanks are due to the following for the use of copyright material:

'New Education' for an extract from an article by A. W. Rowe; Education Department, County Council of Essex, for an extract from the Report 'Counselling and the Child Guidance and School Psychological Services'; Houghton Mifflin Company for an extract from *Man in a World at Work*, ed. H. Borow; The National Foundation for Educational Research, Slough, for extracts from P. P. Daws' article 'What Will the Counsellor Do?'

PART ONE THE SOCIAL CONTEXT

1. Guidance, Counselling and Social Needs

Maurice Craft

School systems, though they may express the qualities of individual teachers, administrators and politicians, and while they may develop autonomous organisational characteristics, are fundamentally shaped by *societal* forces. This broad generalisation underlies the discussion in this opening chapter which will attempt to sketch some aspects of the social context in which the appointment of counsellors in British schools has arisen.

But first, what do we mean by 'guidance and counselling'? The process has perhaps three generally accepted components—educational guidance, vocational guidance and personal counselling. *Educational guidance* is usually felt to involve advice to pupils, parents and teachers on the choice of courses, in the light of a variety of objective and impressionistic data—test scores, teachers' assessments over a period, classroom performance, emotional adjustment, and level of aspiration. *Vocational guidance* similarly involves a continuous and careful assessment of interest, aptitude, and potential over a period, using a variety of sources of data; together with educational guidance (and in the light of likely career opportunities, and of the help of the Youth Employment Officer) this is perhaps an advance on traditional careers work in schools. *Personal counselling* is related both to educational and vocational guidance; but it is also concerned with emotional disturbance and behaviour problems. This area of the school counsellor's work is likely to involve him or her in contact, not only with parents and other teachers, but also with a variety of outside welfare specialists in child guidance, child care, probation and so on.

This is merely a very brief outline of the range of responsibilities a school counsellor might have, and they are discussed in more detail by Hugh Lytton in Chapter Seven of this book. There are however several further points which ought just to be mentioned. First, the amount of time a counsellor might spend on any of these three aspects of his work might vary a great deal from school to school, as indeed is illustrated by the case studies reported in the Schools Council Working Paper on *Counselling in Schools*, which was published last year (Schools Council, 1967).

Second, that while there might be slightly more emphasis on *advice-giving* in educational and vocational guidance, the general approach to all three areas of the counsellor's work would be 'non-directive'; rather than handing a child a ready-made solution, the counsellor would be more concerned to develop the child's own capacity for decision-making. And third, the counsellor is basically concerned with the *prevention* of behaviour or personality problems, and with the *anticipation* of educational and vocational decisions. The counsellor is not primarily a diagnostician to be called in when there is trouble; nor is he an advice-giver on courses and careers, to be consulted on the last day of term. His involvement is a continuing one, and it clearly requires the development of accurate and comprehensive school records.

These are the kinds of activities in which counsellors in schools in the United States are traditionally engaged, and it is a pattern which our schools will probably follow for some years at least. How has this development arisen in British schools? What social needs is it designed to meet?

Guidance, and the growth of an egalitarian political ideology

Perhaps one of the most striking contextual pressures of post-war years has been the growth of an egalitarian political ideology. The welfare state, of course, has origins dating back well beyond 1945, but perhaps few would deny that its most massive provisions were devised and enacted by the Attlee government of the immediate post-war years. A socialist ethic, placing emphasis on the extension of individual freedom through the intervention of the state, enlarged educational opportunities, and implemented basic rights to health, housing, employment, and so on.

These measures were gradualist and for the most part have been steadily refined and extended by subsequent governments.

They represent the western liberal tradition at a mid-point somewhere between the rather more competitive individualism of North America and the rather more pronounced collectivism of parts of Europe. But as a number of writers have noted, the effect of post-war 'democratisation' has been reflected in educational changes in *most* European countries (Reuchlin, 1964, chap. 1).

Increased security of employment, the effect of fiscal and welfare legislation, and rising living standards have been associated with an increased demand for extended education* and a greater participation by working class children in selective secondary education. There is a sense in which all this can be seen as being related to the prevailing political ideology of post-war Britain (Halsey, 1961, chap. 1).

The sequence of reports from the Central Advisory Council— *Early Leaving* (1954), 'Crowther' (1959), 'Newsom' (1963), and 'Plowden' (1967); the 'Robbins Report' (1963), and the successive sociological enquiries (e.g. Mays, 1962; Douglas, 1964; Bernstein, 1965), which have illustrated the still very marked variations in life-chance between children at different social levels, have acted as both cause and effect of the continuing concern to democratise our educational system.

The development of guidance and counselling, I suggest, is in the same tradition. The counsellor is a facilitator whose concern is with the individual, regardless of background; a source of guidance and information where necessary (and for the very large numbers of families without experience of extended and of selective education this is very necessary); and a source of skilled help where stresses associated with social mobility arise.

If we consider the special problems of the 'educational priority area', the concern a democratic society feels for the under-privileged is perhaps reflected in the appointment of school counsellors, school social workers, teacher/social workers, and similar specialists, whose function is largely personal counselling and contact with parents and neighbourhood welfare agencies.

To return to the democratisation of the school system, it might be argued that the growing criticism of *streaming* is again a reflection of the prevailing political ideology; recent studies indicate that the early tracking-off of children into distinct and separate routeways through the primary and secondary school can lead to a polarisation of abilities and attitudes, and perhaps

* The figures are given by Daws (1968), p. 40.

to a needless depressing of the self-concept for a majority of children (Douglas, 1964; Hargreaves, 1967). Similarly, it could be argued that the abandonment of selection at eleven-plus for a tripartite system, and the substitution of more comprehensive systems with delayed selection, easier transfer, and more flexible groupings similarly relate to a more egalitarian ethical view. The examination of the public school system by a Royal Commission (Weinberg, 1967, chap. 1); the reassessment of the role of the universities and of their financial autonomy; the relationship of curriculum reform to the raising of the school leaving age (and the need, that is, to come to terms with the interests and outlook of the working class adolescent)—all these developments might be viewed as educational consequences of our evolving ethical system.

Whether or not one accepts this particular interpretation, there seems little doubt that once selection at eleven-plus has been postponed to the age of thirteen, fourteen or fifteen years, and once the eleven-plus decision has been replaced by one involving a far more extended form of assessment, the need for skilled guidance and counselling becomes urgent. Once the tripartite system has been superseded by a pattern of larger schools, more differentiated curricula and more flexible groupings the need for educational guidance and for personal counselling seems to follow automatically. The school counsellor can provide *globality of concern* (Daws, 1967, p. 85), an all-round view of the whole child in his total social setting, and not merely a snapshot of the part which shows during arithmetic or history or P.E.; as schools become larger and organisationally more complex this becomes increasingly important, as does the need for someone to *co-ordinate* the efforts of the teaching staff and of outside welfare specialists in case of need. As Peter Daws (1967) has written, it is difficult for the headteacher always to do this; and the organisational demands being made upon headteachers will continue to grow, leaving them less and less time in which to do it.

However, persuasive as this kind of speculation might be, there are alternative views on how and why guidance and counselling has arisen in British schools. For example, it has been suggested that advanced industrial societies are *anxiety prone* by virtue of their predominantly urban nature, their rapid rate of social change, their cultural pluralism (i.e. the variety of moral codes they manifest); because of the decline of the large, extended family, the increased rate of geographical and social mobility, the influence of the mass media, and so on. And if all this is true, then perhaps the appointment of counsellors is some kind of psycho-therapeutic response to acute social need.

I doubt if this is a view which could be sustained without a great deal of clarification and qualification; but I would suggest a third view on why guidance and counselling has arisen in British schools which may be well worth our considering. This is the suggestion that while the educational system clearly interacts with the prevailing political ideology (in the way indicated above) it also interacts with the *economy*.

Guidance, and Britain's post-war economic crises

If the rise of an egalitarian political ideology in post-war years has been one very important influence on the development of guidance and counselling in British schools, our continuing economic crises have probably constituted a second. From this point of view, the Reports of the Central Advisory Council, the 'Robbins Report', the sociological studies referred to above, all can be seen as reflecting anxiety about the *waste of talent* as a result of unsupportive (and often impoverished) home backgrounds; waste of talent through streaming in the primary school, rigid selection at eleven-plus, deterioration in the grammar school, and early leaving. The under-representation of working class (and especially lower working class) children in selective secondary and higher education (in view of the greater *absolute* numbers of very able children in the working class) might be interpreted as a major source of national weakness in our economic difficulties.

The concern to involve parents, to raise aspirations and reduce under-achievement, to improve teaching techniques and the structure of the curriculum, might all be considered to demonstrate concern with educational productivity. Indeed, we have recently seen attempts to measure the productivity of secondary schools (Blaug and Woodhall, 1968), and this year's Universities' Conference was on the theme *Universities and Productivity* (Universities' Conference, 1968).

Some commentators give considerable pre-eminence to the influence of economic factors on educational change. William

Taylor (1968), for example, relates the way in which we *define ability* to changes in the occupational and social structure, in the following words:

> In the restrictive economic environment of the 'thirties the psychological rationalisation of existing patterns of educational provision in terms of hereditary endowment no doubt served its purpose. But today, when skill is scarce and educability at a premium, the more hopeful environmentalism of the sociologist is in the ascendant and the psychometrician is in partial eclipse (*op. cit.*, p. 7).

Elsewhere, Taylor (1967) argues that comprehensive education, with its more flexible arrangements for identifying and developing talent, may be a more appropriate response to the changing social structure.

We should probably be safe, for the present, in concluding that the influence of both political ideology *and* of our post-war economic difficulties has influenced the coming of guidance and counselling. As Leona Tyler (1961) has written of the United States, 'It is the combination of an extremely diversified industrial society with democratic ideals that makes counselling necessary'* (*op. cit.*, chap. 1). The trouble is that the kinds of distinctions I have been making are artificial ones, they facilitate analysis but they are unreal. Education, the dominant political ideology, the economy, and the system of social stratification all interact and interpenetrate. Would it be possible, for example, to disentangle the dominant 'laissez-faire' ideology of the Victorian 'golden age' from the highly individualistic form of economic and industrial organisation, and from the stratified class system of that time? Who is to say what *causal relationships* were operating then, or are operating now?

Is our present concern for the individual a *result* of the shortage of skill? And is the humanitarian justification of comprehensive education and of guidance and counselling a corollary of the balance of payments problem? Or do our economic problems *arise out of* an imperfect egalitarianism, an inefficient talent search, wasteful and unproductive educational practices? The pattern of things that is only now beginning to change?

The relationship of educational change to the wider social structure is always an extremely complex one and simple

---

* Ohlsen (1964) makes the same observation, noting too that the counsellor will be concerned about the pupils' mental health as this will affect the efficiency of learning and the realisation of potentialities (*op. cit.*, chap. 1).

explanations are rarely possible. Nor does the meagre literature on the introduction of guidance and counselling into British schools help us very much. What has been written concentrates on defining the rôle of the counsellor, on the principles by which he will operate, and on the techniques which he will use. There is very little societal analysis at all. Peter Daws moves a little in this direction when he refers to the 'continuity of concern' which the counsellor will represent when there is a high teacher turnover (Daws, 1967, p. 84).* The 'educational priority areas' suffer a high staff turnover as we know, and it is far more widespread than that because of the national trend to earlier marriage, more marriage, and earlier child-bearing. But if it is true that these demographic trends are related to increased standards of living in Britain, to what extent does it follow that the appointment of counsellors is a function of an economically determined high rate of staff turnover?

Cicourel and Kitsuse (1963) in their quite critical study of the guidance and counselling system in an American high-school, comment on the boost given to the development of guidance and counselling in the United States as a result of the so-called 'crisis' in American education—the anxiety about falling behind in the east-west race for technological superiority which began when the Russians launched their first 'Sputnik' in 1957.** As the authors say, a great deal of attention has since been devoted to the identification and developing of talent in American schools. But as they also point out, the appointment of such specialists is in line with the progressive differentiation and specialisation of functions and structure which is characteristic of advanced industrial societies.

The relationship of education and the economy

So far, this paper has attempted to outline some of the significant social, economic and political pressures which, I suggest, have created a climate in which guidance and counselling procedures have begun to develop in British schools. It has concentrated on political ideology, economic development, and associated changes in the social structure; but it has also indicated the

* Daws (1968) also offers a brief historical account of the rise of vocational guidance.
** A point discussed more fully in Lytton (1968), chap. 5.

complexity of any such analysis. The next step is to probe the relationship of education and the *economy* a little further. Clearly, we cannot claim any simple causal relationship here (Banks, 1968, chap. 2); but this is not to deny the great importance of the relationship of education with this particular aspect of the social context.

The kind of society we are moving into in the second half of this century has been called the *technological* society. This is the stage of advanced industrialism where, for example, the size of the average manufacturing unit becomes very large; where the importance of new science-based industries grows rapidly (e.g. chemicals, plastics, electrical engineering); and where more emphasis is given to research and development, to new management techniques, to electronic equipment and automation (Musgrave, 1965). This is the phase of industrialism where invention follows innovation at a steadily accelerating pace and where *adaptability* at all levels of the labour force is at a premium.*

The introduction of guidance and counselling in schools, if it contributes to the adolescent's maturity, self-awareness, and 'rôle flexibility' (Davies and Gibson, 1967), will obviously be very relevant to this increasing social need for adaptability.

But the one characteristic of the technological society which cannot escape the attention of anyone working in guidance and counselling is the changing character of the labour force. When a society begins to industrialise it loses workers from the *primary sector* (agriculture, mining) to the *secondary sector* (manufacturing); and as it moves into the advanced phase it begins to develop a sizeable *tertiary sector* (the service occupations such as banking, the professions, and distribution).** In fact the United Kingdom now employs very few people in the primary sector, more than ten times as many in the secondary sector and over eleven times as many in the tertiary sector (Central Statistical

---

* '. . . adaptability is today a good deal more important than a generalised commitment to "hard work", although it is the latter that still features strongly in the ethos of most teachers and schools.' (Taylor, 1967, p. 95.)

** 'This development is illustrated in the growth of the number of such specialists as business-efficiency consultants, labour-managers, time-study engineers, and dieticians, which rose from 6,000 in 1931 to 17,000 in 1951' (Watson, 1964, p. 132). [But over the same period there were significant *decreases* in the numbers of gamekeepers, chimney sweeps, and private detectives (Marsh, 1965).]

Office, 1967).* What is more, within the secondary sector also, administrative, professional and clerical occupations are increasing; and this is the sector where the demand for semi-skilled and unskilled workers is dwindling and that for skilled and technical operatives is growing.** Perhaps two examples, one from the United States and one from Britain, will illustrate these trends:

Between 1940 and 1950, the number of engineers in America is said to have almost doubled, and between 1940 and 1960 the number rose from under 300,000 to 800,000. By 1970, the Bureau of Labor Statistics estimates that there will be a need for about $1\frac{1}{2}$ million engineers (which would amount to an increase of nearly 90 per cent between 1959 and 1970) (Trow, 1963, p. 16).

In Britain, the number of doctors increased by some 90 per cent between 1901 and 1951, but paramedicals (physiotherapists and radiographers for example) increased by 320 per cent in the same period. The ratio of doctors/paramedicals to each member of the population fell from 1:340 to 1:157 over this period (Taylor, 1968, p. 24).

Now bearing in mind what we have said about there being no simple causal relationship between education and the economy, it seems difficult to ignore the parallel development, on the one hand, of the technological society's insatiable appetite for skill, and on the other, the rise of more flexible talent-seeking and talent-generating procedures in schools, of which guidance and counselling may be regarded as one (and of course, the massive growth of the system of public examinations another***).

The relationship between education and the economy, though not a simple one, is clearly of vital importance. The proportion of our gross national product devoted to education has steadily increased, rising from 3·1 per cent in 1952 to 4·7 per cent in 1962 (Poignant, 1967; Vaizey and Sheehan, 1968). Our teaching

* In 1881 (and allowing for imperfections of classification) about 17 per cent of the employed population of England and Wales was occupied in the *primary sector*, about twice as many in the *secondary* sector, and nearly three times as many in the *tertiary* sector. By 1901, the *primary* sector had dropped to 15 per cent, while nearly two and a half times as many worked in the *secondary* sector, and $3\frac{1}{4}$ times as many in the *tertiary* sector. (Marsh, 1965, chap. 5.)

** 'It has been estimated that by 1975 the United States will require 65 per cent more professional and technical personnel than there were in 1960, 51 per cent more service workers, but only 18 per cent more operatives and no addition to the number of labourers.' (Taylor, 1967, p. 90.)

*** (D.E.S., 1960; Campbell, 1968).

force, now over one-third of a million, is one of the largest occupational groups in the country and is still growing. [The figure for America is over 1½ million (Sirjamaki, 1967).] As the 'Robbins Report' has put it, 'the richer a community the more education it wants and can afford' (*op. cit.*, para. 192), and U.N.E.S.C.O. figures seem to bear this out. Expenditure on education in such European countries as Belgium, France, Germany, Italy and Holland in 1962, for example, averaged about 4¼ per cent of gross national product; while the average for such developing countries as Madagascar, Nigeria and Senegal averaged 2·6 per cent a year earlier.* The figure for the United States in 1962 was 5½ per cent (Poignant, 1967).

So Robbins' simple paradox, 'the richer a community the more education it wants and can afford', seems to sum up this part of the argument very neatly. As countries become richer the more resources they are able to devote to educational expansion; but the dynamic of the technological society creates such a demand for talent that educational output becomes a *determinant* of further economic progress.

McGee's recent essay on the place of education in social change argues that educational arrangements are sometimes an *agent* of change, sometimes a *condition* of change, and sometimes an *effect* of change (McGee, 1967); and it would be interesting to apply this analysis to the relationship of education and the economy over a particular period of time to see how often or under what conditions education is an *agent* (or 'determinant') of economic change rather than a *condition* or an *effect*. If we were to try the same exercise in relation to some of the other social functions of education—the transmission of values, or preparation for membership of a political democracy, for example— it might help clarify the relative importance of each of these functions and, in particular, to clarify whether the emphasis which is often placed on the *education-economy* link is completely justified.

In this paper I have been discussing the development of guidance and counselling against the vast backcloth of political ideology, social structure and economic change. I have stressed the complexity of the interrelationship of education with these

* These figures exclude foreign aid however: and the quoted *rate of increase* was considerable for both industrialised and developing countries. It is also important to remember that sheer *volume* of investment in education is less significant for economic development than the *kinds* of investment made (Harbison, 1967).

major features of our social system; but I have nonetheless underlined the importance of education's relationship with the economy. I have therefore tended to emphasise guidance (educational *and* vocational) rather than personal counselling, and I think I probably agree with Professor Wiseman's view that:

> An appropriate British system [of guidance and counselling] would avoid [the American] tendency to excessive emphasis on 'depth psychology' and the controversy over 'directive' and 'non-directive' counselling, and would give more weight to the identification of talent and aptitudes, and the tailoring of courses to particular patterns and profiles of abilities, leading up to a soundly-based system of vocational guidance at the end of the secondary school course. (Wiseman, 1964, p. 151.)

At the same time (and leaving aside the special problems of the 'culturally deprived' and multi-cultural neighbourhoods where personal counselling would obviously be important), it is difficult to see how personal counselling *could* be divorced from an essentially talent-generating system. It is not in the United States. The development of *achievement motivation* (the desire to persevere and excel, and to pursue high career aspirations) is an aim of the American counsellor and is largely conducted through the personal interviewing of 'under-achievers' (Cicourel and Kitsuse, 1963).

The relationship of the individual and the state

Finally, an issue which perhaps underlies all the above, and all such discussions of guidance and counselling systems—the relationship of *the individual and the state*.

In considering (earlier on in this paper) the rise of guidance and counselling in British schools as being possibly related to the prevailing *political ideology* of post-war years, the implication was that an egalitarian educational policy is perhaps more concerned with the *individual* than with any benefit the state might derive incidentally. When, however, we considered guidance and counselling as being possibly related to *economic* factors, the implication was perhaps that in this case the benefit of the *state* was the prime aim and that of the individual was more incidental. The question is, where does the school counsellor stand in this? *Can* he (or *should* he) stand in the middle? Is his concern primarily with national needs or individual needs? Let us consider some views on this.

Take, for example, Drucker's comment:

> The highly educated man has become the central resource of today's society, the supply of such men the true measure of its economic, military and even its political potential. (1959)

Or that of Burton Clark:

> In the technological society—the currently most advanced stage of industrialism—highly trained men replace raw materials and the factory machine as the crucial economic resource. (1962)

Such statements as these seem to minimise the role of the individual. The 'Crowther Report' (1959) begins to draw a distinction for us in discussing what it sees as the two purposes of education: education as a basic human right and a social service for which the state must assume responsibility; and education as an investment. These twin purposes, they felt, have varied in emphasis over the years,* but the Committee thought them inseparable; they felt that 'primacy must be given to the human rights of the individual boy or girl. But *we do not believe that the pursuit of national efficiency can be ranked much lower*— not least because without it the human rights themselves will not be secure.' (My italics. *Op. cit.*, para. 86.)

The 'Robbins Report' (1963) seemed to find a way out of this apparent dilemma which is in some ways perhaps typical of its time. Education, the Committee thought, is clearly an investment in a nation's future; but, they observed, 'the goal is not productivity as such but the good life that productivity makes possible' (*op. cit.*, para. 621). This seems to imply that we pursue productivity *first*, and that from the profit of our labours we then seek individual happiness.

Somewhat unexpectedly, it might be thought, it is among the educational planners and the sociologists that we find some of the strongest views on the *individual* side of the equation. Raymond Poignant of the International Institute for Educational Planning, for example, writes that educational planning involves the moulding of educational output to match the estimated trends in the adult occupational structure. This, of course,

* Gerald Bernbaum (1967) discusses a similar conflict of views current much earlier in this century. The 'Dainton Report' appears to indicate the same balance of view in para. 3. (Council for Scientific Policy, 1968, chap. 1.)

assumes that individuals will make decisions which conform to national needs. But this necessity to match educational output with national needs, Poignant says, 'does not mean that guidance is to be coercive'. In fact, he continues, experience shows that when new courses or new schools are set up the provision of adequate vocational information to students and their parents is usually sufficient to orient students in the direction sought.* But if this does *not* prove sufficient, 'it is up to the government through its incentives policy (particularly . . . by influencing wage levels and giving priority when granting scholarships) to get the sort of orientation it wants' (1967, p. 49). In other words, the rôle of the state in our culture is to encourage and entice the flow of talent, but not to direct it.

Beeby of Harvard, another educational planner, has stated quite explicitly that the rights of the individual child must be paramount. 'The new techniques in planning,' he writes, 'have, if anything, intensified the need for the educational watchdog' (1967, p. 24).

Lastly, Ronald Corwin (1965) goes even further, and questions the morality of the current American anxiety to enrol all able students in higher education. Are we not assuming, he observes, 'that all who can benefit also wish to, or that they should be so enticed, or that college would be to their benefit regardless of their wishes'. And he goes on: 'To the extent that talented persons have no inclination to capitalise on their talent, a national policy which utilises talent as a basis for guiding persons into jobs is as arbitrary in its way as ascription at birth formerly was' (*op. cit.*, p. 200). He even suggests that it might be wiser to concentrate on training the highly *motivated* student rather than trying to motivate the highly *talented* one. Trying to motivate the talented (which may be one of the counsellor's tasks) can lead to his alienation from peer group, family and neighbourhood. But concentrating on the highly motivated would satisfy the national need for trained personnel without violating the integrity of the individual, and it would, he claims, be more efficient (*op. cit.*, chap. 7).

Or as Halsey (1961) has put it: 'Ultimately we must be prepared to recognise that an educational system which was closely and completely geared to supplying manpower for the productive organisation of society would, at the same time, be an agency of

* A point made also by Anderson (1967) who appears somewhat sceptical of guidance (*op. cit.*, p. 23).

dehumanisation . . . beyond acquiring the necessary moral and cognitive equipment to enable him to live in a complex society, a man or woman has the right *not* to be educated and certainly the right not to be trained for a job or career according to the passing requirements of the national economy. The arrangements of society for the production of skill and wealth must, in the last analysis, take their place as means to the end of an enriched life for the individual citizen.' (*Op. cit.*, p. 20.)

Now these are a section of views on the relationship of the individual and the state, with particular reference to the development of guidance and counselling systems; and they range from the conception of education as *talent production* through to a far more highly individualistic perspective. How do we reconcile the conflicting principles? What should our policy be? Perhaps the question should be, 'What are the *fixed points* in this situation, and how much scope for manoeuvre do we actually have?' *Do we have any choice*, to put it simply? For if a technological society has the *structural imperatives* I have described—the expanding tertiary sector, the rapid social change, the need for adaptable, creative people in ever-increasing numbers—then perhaps we should accept that education is concerned with the state and not with the individual.

But I do not believe that this corollary is true. There is little doubt that the structural imperatives exist; that technological societies (in whatever continent and under whatever flag) feed on skill, that they are *élitist* in the sense that they need to select the ablest to fill positions of responsibility, and that they are *egalitarian* in that they need to search everywhere for the ablest. These are the fixed points, common to all such societies. But their *moral imperatives* may differ. The west has a more individualistic culture than the newer industrial societies of the east; its élitism is still rigid and its egalitarianism incomplete, so that the identification and development of talent is much less efficient than it might be. But it allows far greater freedom of choice to the individual at every level, and the price which is paid for this individualism is often felt to be well worth it in terms of the associated social and political benefits.

The development of guidance and counselling in British schools, therefore, can be seen to be related to a variety of mid-twentieth-century social, political, and economic developments of which the growth of the economy is probably the most significant. But guidance and counselling, because of its key rôle in relation both to *the economy* and to *individual life-chances*, treads an extraordinarily difficult path. As a specialised technique of considerable range and depth, it has enormous liberative potentialities for the individual boy or girl, as well as for the state. But like all such techniques it has equally great potentialities for rigidifying the new openness of secondary education (Taylor, 1967, p. 97), for closing doors, for pressuring the individual child, and for the invasion of privacy*—all in the cause of talent production.

To my mind, there is every reason for moving on with this exciting new development which can enrich both the state and the life of the individual. But as a democratic society we must recognise the risks.

---

* Consider, for example, Cicourel and Kitsuse's disturbing comment: 'We do not doubt that from a psychiatric point of view the behaviour of some students may be diagnosed as serious problems that call for specialised treatment, but these students must certainly represent a small fraction of the student population. We do question, however, the propriety of a procedure that routinely assigns students to counselors who not only monitor their progress but actively seek and probe for "problems". This is an invasion of privacy, however disguised it may be by an ideology of service and "help", and an invasion during a period when maintaining the privacy of unique personal experience may be critical for the adolescent's awareness of his own individuality. What is even more disturbing is the prospect that this solicitous treatment will produce a new generation of youth socialised to the practice of easy confessions and receptive to "professional" explanations of who they are and what they aspire to become.' (*Op., cit.* p. 147.)

A Comment on Chapter One

Robin Pedley

Mr. Craft's clear, balanced analysis provided the conference with an excellent base from which members could, and did, launch their own reflections and theories. This brief comment is merely one of the many responses which Mr. Craft's address provoked.

Hitherto, the need in England for school counselling as it is now understood has been severely restricted by our rigid social and educational system. This system bears a nineteenth-century railway character: fixed tracks along which the upper class, middle class and working class go their respective ways *via* 'public', grammar and secondary modern schools respectively. In these schools such factors as pupils' aptitudes, parents' aspirations, and length of schooling have largely been assumed or pre-determined. Teachers as well as pupils are recruited to fit into the prescribed features of the schools. Because the nature and course of the normal educational journey are taken for granted, any guidance which may be needed is done incidentally by teachers, the by-product of whatever information and experience they happen to have acquired.

Just as rail gives way to the greater flexibility and individual convenience of roads (which today also carry most of our goods traffic), so our rigid educational system is being broken up, and replaced by comprehensive schools. A comprehensive school is a school for the whole local community—all social classes, all types of aptitude and ability, and involving parents as well as children. Far from imposing uniformity, as its opponents allege, it is designed to cater for the great variety of individual differences. The curriculum is necessarily richer and more flexible than that provided in the 'limited range' schools previously mentioned.

The more complex your traffic system, the greater is the need for clear, informed guidance throughout. How much more complex is one's journey through any human society! The need for skilled counselling has always been there, in any type of school; the comprehensive school has made the case for it overwhelming. The things that matter most in the comprehensive school—for example, concern for every individual child, the involvement of parents, co-operative planning and participation inside and outside the school—cannot be properly realised without a nucleus of trained advisers. The administrators may create a machine which is *capable* of working efficiently; it is for the counsellors to ensure that human problems do not jam the works, and that students and staff are helped to operate with maximum happiness and achievement.

Should counsellors aim at fitting boys and girls into the existing social order, or on occasion help them to develop in directions which might be regarded by many as anti-social? Given a highly competitive society, with parents and employers demanding success in traditional terms, is there a place in the state school for a counsellor who shares the views of A. S. Neill? Is the counsellor, when the chips are down, the servant of the state or of the individual? Certainly it is imperative that counsellors should be aware of such critical questions, and seek a philosophy of life which will help them to discharge their great responsibilities with humility as well as wisdom. Some may feel that, without compromise or evasion, it is possible to reconcile the seeming opposites posed here. Society, like all living things, must change in any case; and perhaps the true rôle of counsellor and teacher is simply to help every student to be equipped to take his own decisions about the direction and pace of change in his own world. We may agree with this: but does such a conclusion not mean that we are siding firmly with a liberal view of man and his social and educational needs? The fact is that we cannot escape personal responsibility for whatever position we take up. Any training course for counsellors will be deficient if it does not give plenty of scope for the discussion of principles and philosophies in addition to the understanding of individual problems and the practice of techniques.

The need for counsellors in the schools of Britain is manifest. Despite our current economic difficulties, which are holding back this development among others, we can be optimistic about the supply of social and educational workers in the future. As Mr. Craft explains, technological progress will make possible a progressive shift of the labour force from primary and secondary forms of production to services of various kinds. The long record of history shows that, given the opportunity, man is able (in Sir Edward Boyle's words) 'to acquire intelligence'; there is no limit to the pool of ability. We can look forward to a persistent increase in the proportion of people who work in the social field. In short, not only does the social need for school counsellors exist; it will be met—though more slowly than many of us would like.

PART TWO   THE COUNSELLOR AND THE SCHOOL

2. The School Counsellor from the Local Education Authority's Viewpoint

Raymond Gawthorpe

One of the major principles enunciated by the Fulton Committee on the Civil Service was that we should 'look at the job'. Contrary to the opinion of some, we who are engaged in the administrative side of education find it difficult to administer something we know little about. But if one 'looks at the job' of the counsellor one is likely to become bewildered by the different interpretations put upon it. Further enquiry reveals that there are at least three different jobs—personal counselling, educational counselling and vocational counselling. One also quickly realises that there are as many approaches to counselling as there are counsellors, that each brings something of himself to the job. If then one permutates these personal characteristics with the different forms of counselling the possibilities are infinite. Unless, therefore, one defines the job in woolly, generalised terms, the principle of first looking at it does not seem to work. I think I know what a counsellor is; but the only definition of counselling I can give is that it is what a counsellor *does*. By this I mean that it is the work which a trained colleague carries out, in the context of his own school, in co-operation with the rest of the staff and the 'external' agencies. To some extent the work of the counsellor is limited by what other people—pupils, parents, staff, psychologists and so on—allow him to do. I believe that a counsellor succeeds or fails, not by a measure of his work, but by the measure of other people's attitudes towards that work.

Now these comments are not as irrelevant as they may seem, for I like to know what I am dealing with. On counselling I am not yet sure, for as I see it, we are at the moment endeavouring in some degree to transplant an American high school concept into an English secondary school system. And we are doing this, probably with justification, at a time when the secondary schools are undergoing a revolution. Comprehensive education, whether we like it or not, means large schools. Large schools have the danger of becoming impersonal schools, or we fear they may. A good deal of thought has been given to the 'pastoral' care of the student and I have seen the housemaster tutor group system working splendidly. The question is how does the counsellor fit into such an organisation?

The problems are many. Some are personal, others are practical. The personal problems, in my experience, lie almost wholly within the school, but not entirely. Firstly the head himself must be convinced, and must be prepared to make quite significant adjustments. Some, I am sure, sent teachers on 'guidance' courses in the early years without any clear conception of what it was all about. I do not think we can blame them, for few of us were much wiser at the time. On the return of the teacher, fired with a missionary zeal, the head may well have felt that he had got more than he had bargained for! Some indeed, and I have met assistant teachers of the same opinion, saw the counsellor as something of a threat. As one head said to me, 'he'll be sitting in my chair next'. The English tradition of the head as 'father of his flock' is deeply rooted, and has I believe been a good tradition. However, in the larger school, running at around a thousand students, knowing each one individually is just not possible. Hence the delegation to housemasters and others. But housemasters represent the 'establishment', they represent order and discipline. The counsellor represents none of these things. The principle of confidentiality (overdone I feel by some counsellors) is a new one and it may breed suspicion. I once asked a high school principal, in Maryland, 'Are you happy that there are things going on in your school which you do not know about, and, what is more, cannot be told about?' The answer—'Entirely. I must trust my counsellors.' In America such a reply comes automatically. In England, how many heads are ready to give it? And yet without a complete willingness to trust to this degree, for there can be no half measure, counselling is a 'non-starter'.

Secondly, there are the other people to be converted. One of the major problems of introducing a counsellor into a school is that his job, whatever he may make of it, is already to a greater or lesser degree being done by other people. I recall one school where the senior mistress was outraged when misbehaving girls were sent to the counsellor rather than to her. And another where the Education Welfare Officer protested when the third boy from a 'problem home' was dealt with by the counsellor after repeated truancy. His elder brothers had been truants in their time and the Welfare Officer had dealt with them. I recall the occasion on which a counsellor, after testing a student, sent for the parents and told them she should transfer to a grammar school. He arranged for them to see a grammar school head and the first his own head knew about it was a telephone call from the grammar school. It is not enough to say that a modicum of diplomacy could have avoided such situations, something more fundamental is called for. To launch a counsellor into an unprepared situation is asking for trouble. I have pondered often on how one prepares the situation. It helps, I think, if the counsellor returns to the school from which he is seconded, if he is · one whom his colleagues respect both as a person and as a practitioner. The task of 'selling' oneself and 'selling' counselling at the same time is a hard one. Students, on the other hand, take to counselling quite readily. With some, of course, it is a 'try on' and the counsellor must have sufficient wit and experience to spot them, or risk ridicule at the hands of the teaching staff. The majority, in these days when communication with adults is difficult for so many reasons, have a real need for 'someone to talk to'—by which they usually mean someone who will listen to them. Parents I have found uniformly approving. They need someone with whom to share their problems; some indeed are willing to hand over their problems. But the press, perhaps because the job is difficult to define, are no help. The headline 'Counsellor to help girls with their love lives' infuriated me, simply because it was, as far as it went, true.

The practical problems are no less difficult. For example, what is to be the nature of the appointment? Is it to be full-time, or part-time? Should a counsellor serve one school or several? If it is hard to define the job, then the answers to these questions are far from obvious. The teacher/counsellor rôle seems to me a peculiarly difficult one. As a teacher he must represent and exercise discipline; as a counsellor he cannot, not at least in the same terms. Can one be two different people to one student? One needs to think about this from the counsellor's point of view as well as the student's. Sharing a counsellor among two or more schools has its attractions: it makes the service nominally available to more students, and no one minds about an increase of, say, ·3 on a school establishment, whilst an increase of 1 (and that not a teacher) might cause eyebrows to rise, particularly in the context of teacher shortage. But if there is a job to be done, has not any school enough work to keep a counsellor fully occupied? Will not diversification diminish the service? Do problems improve with keeping until the counsellor calls? The difficulty, I should have thought, was the other way about. If a counsellor concentrates, say, on personal counselling, is he not likely to discover a need which is beyond the resources of the psychologists and others to whom it would be made known? As an American counsellor commented, 'Once I think of treatment I am wrong.' What else can the counsellor do but pass on the student for treatment to those qualified to give it? Yet the child guidance services are already overstrained.

I believe that within the next decade local education authorities will have to crystallise their attitudes towards counsellors. They, and the schools, will have to make up their minds to accept counselling, reject it, or modify it, and a good deal of rethinking about staff deployment will be necessary. One of the most interesting discoveries I made during my stay in Maryland was on this very point. There, the counsellor's 'load' in a senior high school (pupils aged sixteen to eighteen years) was three hundred. A school of 1,800 therefore had six. Counting these together with the full-time school nurse, the non-teaching vice-principals, and the librarians, the staff-student ratio was 1:18·5. The *teacher*-student ratio was 1:25·5. I feel that this is imperfectly understood in England. The price of these desirable additions is, quite simply, larger classes. You do not get both, it is either one or the other. Too many teachers, in my view, want these counsellors, librarians, nurses and so on, and want no increase in class size. The Americans have, perhaps more realistically, 'looked at the job'. In England one of the messages none of us can have failed to hear is that education has, at the moment, just about as large a share of the national 'cake' as it is going to get. The appointment of a counsellor to every three hundred students is not practicable in financial terms, even if the universities could train counsellors in the required numbers. Yet the American high school and college system is such that vocational counselling, as we understand it in the careers advisory service, is not a major need. So we have the dilemma of a single-handed counsellor working in an English school, carrying two, three or even four times the student load, and endeavouring to work in a significantly wider field. In the name of experiment, are we not in danger of developing an amateurish approach to something which is strictly the sphere of the professional? If, by some means, we can establish counselling on a professional basis, then clearly a career structure must be created. This is not straightforward if one is to avoid unfavourable comparisons with other members of staff.

How, for instance, do you know whether counselling in a particular school is a success? How do you evaluate it? I remember a counsellor from Southern California telling me, 'My job is to keep them in school.' It was a socially underprivileged area, where the 'drop-out' was not only a social and educational failure, but was virtually certain to fall to temptations which would bring him in conflict with society and the law. On this thesis, sound as it is, success on the counsellor's part could be measured numerically. The fewer the drop-outs the greater the success. But American teachers have another term—'the sit in'—the student who, in their view, ought to have 'dropped out' and has not, who stays at school not because he wants to, but because social and economic factors compel him to, who makes as little effort as he can get away with, and conforms only to the minimum. I have seen such students and doubted whether the situation, either for them or for their teachers, was a fruitful one. What happens then to the evaluation?

One of the more frustrating aspects of my visit to America was my inability to be present at counselling sessions with students. There were entirely proper reasons against such intrusion, but I had a great longing to know what was going on. I could only observe from the outside and I was not always happy with what I saw, though I was heartened by the note sent by a counsellor to a teacher—'All this young man needs is discipline. I cannot give it to him, but I trust you will.' What I did see was that many counsellors spent a good deal more time dealing with paper than dealing with people. The credit system, graduation requirements, exchange of 'transcripts', allied to the mobility of student population made this unavoidable. Dealing with the college applications of three hundred students, each of whom may apply to a dozen or more colleges, administering the college entrance tests and so on is a formidable task in itself. But apart from the needs of a sixth form college where something of this kind may well be necessary, I do not think this is how most of us see the job of a counsellor in England.

Assume, for the moment, that counselling were to be accepted as 'a good thing'. On the counsellor-student load of 1:300, I would need for Hampshire something in the region of eighty counsellors. The universities cannot produce them, but suppose they could? Are there sufficient candidates of the right calibre to train? What is the 'right calibre'? In the United States many more teachers have a knowledge of counselling than are counsellors and the climate of opinion is a favourable one. I am quite sure that when we seriously contemplate training courses for heads and senior staff, counselling and guidance will have to be included. I have often met the demand for one-term courses, the argument being that many more teachers could thereby be trained, that the loss to the school of teaching power would be reduced, and so on. The university departments on the other hand have talked of a two-year postgraduate course. Clearly these are two different things. How then does one select the people? I am sure that local education authorities would like to be consulted more than they are about those who are admitted to these courses. But does a recommendation carry any weight unless one knows what one is recommending for?

Finally, there are purely practical considerations. If the counsellor has come to stay he must have proper working conditions and assistance. He needs his own office, pleasantly furnished, in which he can see students with dignity and privacy. He needs a secretary, preferably in an office connected to his own room. He needs a telephone, quite possibly with its own line, and these are all expensive provisions to make. I personally know of no counsellor who has been given such working conditions, and this, in itself, is a measure of the problem. Every high school I visited in Maryland had its own suite of offices for the counsellors and their secretariat. The demand for ancillary help in schools, particularly for school secretaries, is interminable. Would provision of this kind in our schools help to solve the problem, or aggravate it?

In my own Authority we have endeavoured to find solutions to these problems. We have made our mistakes and learnt from them. But we are not home and dry yet by any means and I have refrained from offering solutions, or conclusions. Professor Moore, of the State University of New York at Buffalo, once said, 'Counselling comes in when choice has to be made.' Before long a choice will have to be made about counselling. We need guidance; perhaps we may find it together.

3. The School Counsellor from the Headteacher's Viewpoint—I*

A. W. Rowe

Headteachers have far more power in this country than in any other: the best headteachers run the best schools, and so on all the way down the line. This is one of the great strengths and at the same time one of the great weaknesses of our tradition. This statement is an over-simplification, no doubt, but it contains a truth that must be taken into account in any realistic thinking about counselling in schools. All headteachers are very conscious of the power they wield and look askance at anything they think might interfere with it. Quite rightly, for the good school is as good as it is simply because the maximum freedom has been granted to the head to run it as he thinks fit.

The reluctance of some headteachers to accept that schools, either singly or in groups, would benefit from having counsellors —as my own experience has convinced me they would—stems to a certain extent from the fact that they think their own power might as a consequence be curtailed. To take an everyday instance; there will be occasions when a counsellor can only do good on the basis that what passes between him and a particular pupil is confidential, not to be told to anyone else, including the headteacher. What a potential threat to the headteacher's total control of his school this could be taken to be. Quite the reverse is the truth, but headteachers have to be convinced. Their reluctance also quite properly stems from the fact that they are not yet sure that a counsellor, particularly when as in my own school he is counted against the establishment, is worth having. They are not yet sure, that is, on purely educational grounds.

Headteachers with such doubts could make a start by reading the growing corpus of writing, both theoretical and practical,

* Some parts of this article previously appeared in *New Education*, February 1968, and are reprinted with the kind permission of the editor.

by British authors. That it is growing is to be welcomed, first, because it is a reflection of the increasing importance of the subject; second, because it does in fact give headteachers the opportunity to read up the subject and make up their own minds about it.

A word of warning. School counselling is still in its youth in this country. The necessary task that the British theorists are undertaking is attempting to define the rôle or rôles counsellors are playing, or will play, in British schools. For though we have turned to the United States for guidance and, perhaps unfortunately to a lesser extent, to Scandinavia, educational ideas and practices do not transplant—or if they do they grow into different kinds of plants. We still have to find out what kind of plant ours is growing into, and just as urgently to keep debating what kind of plant it *should* grow into.

The difficulty of the theorist's task can be illustrated by glancing at the content of the courses for training counsellors now being run at the universities of Keele, Reading, Swansea and Exeter.* These cover a great deal of very varied ground simply because no one yet knows what rôles counsellors in our schools will in fact be called upon to play. The attempt has therefore to be made—and in a one-year course only—to equip them to play as many rôles as possible, even though some of these rôles, in the present opinion of those running the courses, counsellors should not properly be asked to play. The dilemma is a very real one: unless counsellors can prove their value in schools by coping with whatever tasks headteachers allot them, then the general acceptance of the necessity for counsellors will be delayed, perhaps even halted altogether. This would be a great pity.

The theorist's task will be helped as more practical accounts of what counsellors are actually doing in the schools become available. Such accounts will also be valuable to headteachers—to those who already have counsellors working in their schools, to those who are contemplating appointing counsellors, but most of all to those not yet convinced they ought to have them.

Here is one such practical account. It is presented warts and all, because in this context mistakes are as important as successes. The literature on counselling is written, as one would expect, in the specialised vocabulary of the educational psychologist and

* And those for other school welfare rôles being offered at Edge Hill and other colleges of education.

sociologist; 'continuity of concern', 'globality of concern', 'active client participation', 'preventive orientation'—all are headings in a recent illuminatingly-balanced lead article in a symposium, *The Counsellor Function* (Daws, 1967), but I hope I shall be forgiven if I stick to workaday English to describe what is a workaday experiment.

A headteacher who decides to have a counsellor on his staff, especially when this is counted against his establishment, will do so in response to important pupil-needs which are not being met and which he believes will most satisfactorily be met by a counsellor. What these needs are will depend upon the total resources he has at his disposal to satisfy all the educational needs of his pupils. The rôles the counsellor will play will be those necessary to meet the unsatisfied needs. And as the school's total resources develop and change, so must the counsellor's rôles. Part of the interest in our experiment lies just here: it has been running long enough for the counsellor's rôles to have changed—adjusted, perhaps, is the better word—in response to development and change elsewhere in the school.

The school, a purpose built all-through mixed comprehensive school, opened with 1,350 pupils in September, 1964. It is in the main a neighbourhood school, though the bulk of its selective entry comes from housing estates further afield because the area does not throw up enough 'selective' pupils to make a viable comprehensive intake. A part of the neighbourhood is such that we expected (and received) a number of socially-handicapped pupils.

One of the rôles, if not the chief one, that some theorists see school counsellors playing is that of educational and vocational guide. This could well provide more than enough work for a counsellor in anything but a smallish school. The assumption behind this is that either there is not already in the school a careers department, or the careers department is not effectively carrying out its job of educational and vocational guidance. This rôle was not open to our counsellor: the establishment of a strong careers department had been one of our first aims. Note, though, that we have recently changed the name from Careers Department to Educational and Vocational Guidance Department. This reflects a change in our thinking. 'Careers guidance' is too narrow a concept for what we are now doing. There was unfortunately a built-in assumption that it was something that began only in the third or fourth year, and that it was confined only to careers. Whereas educational and vocational guidance begins, or should begin, from the moment a pupil enters the school, and should be a continuous process until the day he leaves. In this process, under the aegis of the EVG department itself, all members of staff—form tutors, subject tutors, and heads of house—should play a conscious part.

The head of our EVG department teaches for only a third of his time, and the second in the department for only two-thirds. Others have specific responsibilities in the EVG team: the senior mistress and the deputy head look after college and university entrants, and entrants into the professions; the head of commerce, secretarial and business careers; the sixth form tutors, the general academic guidance of sixth formers; and the head of the Core Course and her team the careers of Easter and summer leavers.

When we first opened, specific educational guidance began in the third year. It still does, with the recent important addition mentioned below, and is as continuous as we can make it. It is the responsibility of the senior mistress as director of studies, and is linked with the subjects the pupils will be allowed to choose to study from the fourth year on. It involves, among other things, parents' meetings and interviews with each third year pupil (and his parents where necessary), all based upon a thorough knowledge of the pupil's problems, progress, and potential obtained from form tutors, heads of departments, and heads of houses. In this the senior mistress is helped by the deputy head and myself.

As the pupil passes into the fourth year and beyond, the special vocational knowledge and guidance he needs is increasingly provided by the specialist members of the EVG team listed above, under the direction of its head. And this vocational guidance, if it is to be realistic, must always be closely linked with educational guidance: 'If you want to be a teacher, then you must begin by getting at least 5 'O' levels. . . .' Indeed, good vocational guidance must inevitably be good educational guidance and should increasingly be used for what it in fact is—the most powerful of all forces in raising educational attainment.

In a comprehensive school in particular, where you are educating everybody, guidance—detailed, careful, continuous, informed—should be the corner-stone upon which all else is built. Guidance in this all-embracing sense now begins in our school from the moment the pupils come into it. Form tutors and heads of house play an important part here, as do the deputy head and myself, while the senior mistress as director of studies has an overall responsibility for their academic progress.

The counsellor has also an important rôle to play. He visits the contributory primary schools at the end of the summer term and consults the headteachers and their staff. His main purpose is to identify and find out as much as possible about the most disadvantaged pupils so that he can begin helping them as soon as they come to us. As the term wears on, form tutors, heads of house and members of the various departments, especially for obvious reasons the Remedial Department, bring to his attention pupils whose backgrounds, for a variety of reasons, they feel need looking into. It is the parents of these pupils, as well as the parents of the others already identified from his consultations with the primary school staffs, that he will begin visiting first.

The importance of these home visits and the links thus established between the parents and himself is great: 'If you want to help Johnnie you've first got to help his parents.' Of such great importance partly because these are the very parents who normally can never be reached by the usual parent-teacher activities, no matter how hard the school tries. I should like to see these home visits extended and, in certain cases, continued as the pupils go up through the school. To this end I have made it possible for an experienced member of the Remedial Department to help with these home visits and with the follow-up work, establishing her as second counsellor. The counselling of these pupils and the home visits now make up one of the chief rôles that the counsellor plays. The fact that the most severely-disadvantaged pupils are identified before they come into the school itself obviously reduces the amount of 'crisis counselling' the counsellor has to do, although in a large comprehensive school this will always be an important rôle.

The Remedial Department, as you would expect, gives priority to the first year pupils needing help. The information it quickly gathers about these pupils is passed to the counsellor. Some of these pupils he will be already counselling, others he will now begin to counsel.

The best kind of counselling for certain of these pupils—in the private face-to-face situation in his room—will be to teach them to read. Here the counsellor's special skills in diagnosing reading difficulties and in teaching reading will be called fully into play. In a big school this work provides the counsellor with another important rôle.

Most of the counselling when the school first opened was inevitably 'crisis counselling'. The pupils became the main responsibility of the counsellor when, because of some crisis or series of crises, they were brought to his attention. This had the unfortunate effect of identifying him too closely in other pupils' minds (and in the minds of some members of staff) with such pupils, an effect which was all the more unfortunate as many of these pupils were about to come up before the courts or were already on probation. Yet I could see no immediate way out of the dilemma. As well as the urgent need to help such pupils for their own sakes, they also had to be helped if they were not to hinder seriously the progress of other pupils. In a streamed school they would mostly find themselves tucked tidily away in the bottom streams. In a non-streamed school such as ours, they would be in mixed-ability forms, only being withdrawn into the remedial department for special help in reading and number if they needed it.

The counsellor's major rôle at that time was a therapeutic one. He accepted the main responsibility for the most severely-deprived and the most seriously-disturbed pupils. His was the main responsibility, but many others were also involved. How this worked can be seen from the following.

We were fortunate in having five specially-designed house blocks as part of the school's facilities, each built to hold three hundred pupils. Under such ideal physical conditions, a head of house and his team of fourteen or fifteen have been able to get to know their pupils intimately, to establish strong links between home and school, and to be responsible for their pupils' welfare and progress. A pupil's house tutor is also his form tutor and will usually teach him. This is fairly easy to arrange because the house tutor group is in fact the form, a mixed-ability group taught as such for the great majority of subjects in the General School (i.e. Years One to Three).

The School Record Card for each pupil is held and maintained by the head of house. This is so designed that most aspects of the pupil's growth and development—personal, social, and academic—can be recorded. Extra information is passed to the head of house from bursar, counsellor, senior mistress, deputy head, and headmaster. In addition, each form tutor keeps a *Confidential Form Log Book*. It contains the tutor's personal observations, embodies other relevant information, and is passed on to the pupil's next form tutor. The log is a current one and by the end of the year a pupil's entry may run to five or six pages.

Under such a system, each pupil is in fact known intimately to the head of house and his team. Apart from anything else, the opportunities for contact are so great. The house is open from eight o'clock in the morning. The pupils' cloakrooms and lockers are there. Some assemblies are held there, and there they dine. During breaks, dinner-hours, and after school, two of its classrooms are used for homework and quiet games, while dancing or some other activity, e.g. play or music rehearsal. may be going on in the dining-space. There parents come to see the head of house in his study, and there all the house social events, parents' evenings, pupils' dances, old people's social service parties, etc., are held.

It soon became plain to us that all this was not enough. Because the school was so big, and because part of its population was drawn from depressed areas, a fair number of its pupils needed more time and attention—and attention of a more specialised kind—than a head of house and his team, even when supplemented by senior mistress, deputy head, and headteacher, all of whom happen to have special interest in disadvantaged pupils, could give them. So it was primarily to help these pupils that our counsellor was first appointed. Care was taken to ensure from the outset that his work was understood and accepted by the staff for what it was, i.e. a strengthening and extension of the pastoral work they were already doing. Just as important were the measures taken to inform the various statutory and voluntary welfare agencies, upon whose co-operation much of the success of his work would depend.

Pupils and parents, too, had to be taught what the counsellor's job was; they will only talk freely and truthfully when they are convinced that they are in the hands of a counsellor, not a teacher, vested with authority not to divulge what he is told to anyone. Only upon this basis can the necessary relationship between counsellor and client be built. As I have said, in order to help pupils one has often to help their parents first. In the direct counselling of pupils and parents there must be uninterrupted privacy. So the counsellor has his own study, with easy chairs, a filing system, a telephone. The telephone is essential, firstly, because the work necessitates frequent contact with outside agencies on behalf of the pupil—school clinic personnel, school attendance and welfare officers, Children's Department officers, psychiatric social workers at the Child Guidance Clinic, probation officers, or the N.S.P.C.C. Secondly, because it has to be used frequently to help the parents—by contacting the Marriage Guidance Council, Citizens' Advice Bureau, National Assistance Board, or police. The fact that the enquiry can be made at once and in the parent's presence is proof that the counsellor will in fact take action and this reinforces the parent's confidence and trust in him.

During the last two years the school has so developed that the number of 'crisis' pupils in the General School has been dramatically reduced. In this advance, the work of the counsellor has undoubtedly played an important part. The reduction has meant that the counsellor has time to turn his attention to a wider range of pupils, as well as to develop his case work with 'crisis' pupils. Even with the amount of educational guidance and pastoral care that we are able to give, we find that crisis counselling of a different kind is at present frequently needed in the fifth year in particular. And this need will increase as more and more pupils stay on beyond the statutory leaving age. Not necessarily because there are more pupils, but because the more effective a comprehensive school is, the greater the number of pupils will be who are the first in their family to stay on. Many will get no positive family support; at best the family is neutral: 'You can stay on if you want to.' This adds to the pupils' burden. They quite understandably doubt their own ability and fear failure; they fear they will let the family down even more than they fear they will let themselves down. Ideally, the counsellor should take these pupils for general studies or discussion periods of some kind so that a link is established. This could lead to pupils seeking advice from the counsellor as well as giving the counsellor an excuse to see them regularly, either individually or in small groups of friends. Usually, the 'crisis' first reveals itself in a drop in effort—homework is a very good barometer here. Usually, too, the director of studies will ask me to have a chat with the pupil, and this gives me an opportunity to call in the counsellor if necessary.

In a large school, even if one were to concentrate only upon the kinds of counselling I have described, there is always far more work than one counsellor can cope with. All that a headteacher can do is to try to decide how the counsellor can spend his time more profitably. Of one thing I am sure: counsellors should have the benefit of the one year's training now provided in the counselling courses at Keele, Reading, Exeter and Swansea, or the educational guidance course at Manchester (one-term courses in 'Linking Home and School' and 'Careers Guidance' are also offered at Edge Hill College of Education). The kind of qualities a head will be looking for in a counsellor are precisely those qualities upon which candidates are selected for the training courses. The courses themselves vary slightly in their emphasis. A headteacher will be able to assess for himself which course is likely to provide him with the counsellor best able to play the required rôles.

4. The School Counsellor from the Headteacher's Viewpoint—II

Helen Whale

Children today seem often to be alarmingly out of touch with the adult world into which they are seeking to grow. Teenagers especially feel cut off from their parents, and find few other grown-ups to whom they can go with problems that are at all personal and intimate. For some lucky ones a wise aunt or understanding elder sister is accessible, but in the very compact family of today this is not always the case. Their parents do not go to church, so there is no link with a minister or priest, nor is there often a family doctor who has known the child over many years. There may be no one to whom a child can talk except his own contemporaries.

Teachers are very willing to try to fill the gap, and do a great deal to do so. They find a real satisfaction in the 'pastoral' side of their work. They make opportunities to get to know their children outside the classroom, and where Form Tutors, Year or House Heads and subject teachers go up the school for as long as possible with their own girls and boys, close links are forged. Even so, teachers are inevitably limited in what they can do. For one thing, they have not the time they need. There is good Biblical authority for leaving ninety-nine sheep in the wilderness and going back to look for the missing one, but you do worry about the ninety-nine. Furthermore, the teacher has a rôle of authority which may well put some children off, or he may be already too closely involved in their difficulties to be able to give advice that will be well received.

All this made us feel at Mayfield the need for extra help from a sort of 'outsider', yet one whom we knew well and could entirely trust. We wanted a person whom the *children* would trust: someone who would like them and sympathise with them, who would seem approachable, yet would be sure to keep matters private, and who would have the training and experience both to recognise their problems and to find the words which would make it possible and bearable to discuss them. We wanted someone whom *we* could trust: who would give the same advice that a wise teacher or parent would have given, or to whom puzzled and anxious teachers and parents could themselves turn. We also wanted our counsellor to be regularly available to give continuing support to the girls growing up at school.

Three years ago we found the right person. She is married and the mother of three small children. She is a graduate and a trained teacher, with some years of teaching experience. She has a diploma in sociology, and also took the Marriage Guidance Council's course in preparation for counselling work. Above all these valuable qualifications, she is the kind of person we all like.

She comes to school once a week, on the same basis as a part-time teacher, and since it all began has brought a colleague with her, so that we now have two counsellor days each week. This, in a school of nearly 2,000 girls, forced us to concentrate the work somewhere, and we decided to start with the 3rd Year. Every 3rd Year form has four or more sessions with the counsellor, and we divide each form into two groups so that numbers are reasonably small. After group talks and discussions, every girl writes for the counsellor a very short and informal account of herself, and each one has a short individual interview. The brief autobiography is a help in keeping records, and from it and from the discussions the counsellor can judge whether a girl needs more individual help. For a few girls in each form a series of longer interviews will follow. Others may want nothing there and then, but an introduction has been made, and at any time in the next years of her school career a girl can ask for an appointment with the counsellor. That they do so is an encouraging sign of their confidence in her. There are also other individual appointments from any age group in the school, made on the advice of the teaching staff. All these appointments are in school time. No one is ever made to see the counsellor if she does not want to go, and it is essential to avoid any idea that it is a punishment for misbehaviour to go to her, even though it is often the most disturbed and therefore disturbing children whom we want the counsellor to try to help.

What do they want to talk about? They don't use the words, but it is about personal relationships. About getting on at home, and the seemingly unreasonable restrictions still imposed by

Mum and Dad on their all-but grown-up daughter. About jealousies towards brothers and sisters, or the demands made by an elderly grandparent in an overcrowded home. And mostly about boy friends and petting and sex. They know, or think they know, the facts, though some old wives' tales do emerge, and they want to go beyond the facts to discuss the feelings.

Does it help them? You cannot measure success in this sort of work. Certainly the girls seem to value the chance to talk about themselves to an interested listener. Some secret worries and anxieties have certainly been dispelled. The chance to let off steam has been a useful safety valve, and some seriously mal-adjusted children, whose parents are perhaps resisting the idea of psychiatric help, can find relief. So can their teachers. The counsellor works in close co-operation with the Child Guidance Clinic, to whom she can refer cases and whose advice she can seek. She is also of course in close touch with the other children's services: Youth Employment Officers, Care Committee, Pro-bation Officers, and so on.

How do the parents react? Occasionally I have had a visit or phone call from a parent who is worried at 'all these prying questions' into family life. An explanation of what the counsellor is really trying to do usually reassures them. Many welcome the help that can be given, for they are as worried as we are when their daughters retreat behind a screen of adolescent sulkiness and seem to be impossible to talk to. Sometimes, in the end, after a series of interviews, a girl will be proud to arrange for her mother to meet the counsellor, either at home or at school.

The teaching staff have welcomed the help of our counsellor, recognising her as a fellow member of staff, even though she is not very much in the staff room, and calling on her special expertise. There could have been jealousies and a resentment of a stranger who appeared to be drawing the girls' confidences away from their teacher, but in a school where we depend tremen-dously on mutual trust and co-operation, where 'empire building' is, we hope, at a minimum, and where Form Tutors in any case take the initiative and much of the responsibility in looking after their own girls, additional help from a counsellor or anyone else has been gladly received.

Nor has the matter of information given in confidence proved to be a difficulty in fact, although in theory the counsellor might find herself burdened with confidences which, in the interests of the girl herself, she felt she should communicate to either another teacher or the parents. To do so would be very damaging, for the slender, tensile thread of trust between counsellor and child will not snap, but can easily be cut. Nothing must be passed on without the girl's own permission. Until she is ready to call in others, the counsellor has to help her face her difficulties alone. In practice, we have found that once a problem has been discussed with the counsellor some of its private horror has gone, the girl herself can view things more objectively, and she is likely to be ready to seek further outside help if this is really necessary.

The new service is proving its worth to us. We see areas where it could be extended, in the first year of secondary school, for example, or in the fifth and sixth with more emphasis than at present on careers advice. For the time being we are glad of what we have. There is not perhaps a great deal that a counsellor can do which could not be done by wise and experienced teachers who had the same time and opportunity: but the wisest and most experienced of our teachers are very glad of her help.

A Comment on Part Two

Paul Kline

Since it is a well-known phenomenon that the enthusiasm for a cult is in inverse proportion to the number of its devotees, delegates to this conference might, perhaps, be excused their assumption that counselling is good and the more the better. Nevertheless, Chapter Two ensures that at least some attention is paid to the undoubted problems of introducing counselling into British schools on anything like a national scale.

One of the points raised is that the counsellor is a threat both to the headteacher and to certain of the staff, for example, the careers teacher. No amount of semantic disputation on the rôle of counsellor, nor the invocation of professional skills to overcome the difficulty can however alter the fact that as long as some headteachers like to take upon themselves the job of counselling their pupils, these same heads will feel threatened because one of their duties is being usurped. Furthermore, as long as English education remains decentralised and headteachers retain their autonomy this problem will remain. Nor is it easy to change the climate of opinion that training is not essential (echoes of Aristotle's flutes) when even counsellor-trainers themselves (as later papers indicate) admit that the personality of the counsellor is a most important variable in the successful counselling situation. The only argument then left is that a good man trained is better than one untrained. Thus, then, as a result of the autonomy of the head of a school the introduction of counselling must depend upon his inclination.

However, the argument that in the present financial situation more counsellors would mean less teachers which the speaker seemed to consider a powerful counterblast against the introduction of counselling seems less convincing. It is clearly only applicable if the mental health of pupils is regarded as less important than instruction in particular subjects. Indeed, it could even be argued that counselling by reducing emotional difficulties would lead to increased academic performance. However, if mental health is regarded as equally or more important than subject teaching such a burden would be willingly borne. It should be pointed out that there is no evidence from America that the introduction of counselling led to greater size of classes and it is well known that the size of sixth form groups in some of the famous direct-grant schools is very large without any apparent deleterious effects on standards. The very existence of this conference and the courses available in counselling are evidence that mental health is regarded as important in education at least by a minority. The power of the weakening of teacher-numbers as an argument against the introduction of counselling is based on a derogation of its importance.

If, however, Mr. Gawthorpe is correct and mental health is a neglected aim of educationists and especially of teachers then, as occurs in America, it would be sensible for teachers to be acquainted with counselling in their training course even if not counselling themselves. This, if there is a good argument for counselling other than the support of vested interests, would bring about the desired climate of opinion and perhaps enable a career structure for counsellors to be set up, the lack of which it was argued contra-indicated the introduction of counselling at this time.

Another point against counselling, it was claimed in this paper, was the deficiency of the school psychological service, which is already overburdened. The counsellor would merely discover more work. However, unless it be argued that counsellors actually create these cases, such problem children must already go undetected. What the counsellor would do would be to select the most severe cases, an occupation for which his training befits him.

The final argument against counselling in this paper begins to overlap with that of the second. Here it was claimed that more teachers would mean less need for counsellors. This, of course, is in another form the headteachers' claim that given the contact and the right personality a teacher can counsel.

Chapter Three is descriptive rather than analytic or theoretical, being an outline of some guidance procedures in a large comprehensive school. The first point to notice is that no attempt has been made to evaluate the results of setting up this counselling service in any systematic way although the school is clearly satisfied with it. Thus, as a model for future development this description must be regarded with some caution. It is of interest to note, with reference to Chapter Two, that this headmaster clearly sees that the counsellor does make inroads on the traditional power of the head of the school. Nevertheless, he also realises that in a large school where the demands for guidance are likely to be great, a trained specialist is needed. For, as is pointed out later, counsellors were appointed because the work became too much for house tutors.

There are a number of interesting features about the guidance services in the school, especially the visits to the local primary schools and to the homes of socially disadvantaged pupils. From the limited evidence available such links would appear to be most valuable. Of course such procedures as entering homes, especially the homes of parents whose views may not be consonant with those of the school, are fraught with danger. Mistakes by the counsellor could perhaps damage the child more than had nothing been done. Training in this work would appear essential. Perhaps even more significant, therefore, is the emphasis Rowe lays on training. To conclude these comments therefore a more general point about training should be made. The skilled practitioner of any profession, trained or not, must do things that the unskilled practitioner does not do. It is the function of training to discover what these things are and thus to teach them and to enable others to do them. If they can only be done by a certain select few by reason of personality or intelligence then selection for such profession has to take these into account. The notion of intuitive skill is conceptually empty and is based on an insufficient analysis of the relevant process. To argue that training is not necessary means that there are no skills involved. Long ago now the Amateurs' gate was closed at Lords: counselling is also important.

PART THREE THE COUNSELLOR AND OUTSIDE AGENCIES

5. The School Counsellor and the Child Guidance Clinic

George Robb

Although I have played a part in the introduction of counselling into Essex secondary schools, I must make it clear that I have no hard evidence to offer on whether counselling, as carried on in Essex, has proved undeniably successful, nor indeed have I current personal involvement in a Child Guidance Clinic. It may, however, be useful to describe the problems occasioned by the attempt to introduce counselling to certain Essex schools, with particular reference to those I encountered initially, with some later statements of the co-operation between an Essex psychologist and the counsellors concerned. That this co-operation takes place almost entirely outside the clinical rôle of the educational psychologist is one result of the attitude of the psychiatrists concerned—but more of this later.

Some time ago I visited Keele University to meet the people training counsellors, and to find out more of the content of the course than was possible by reading the handouts. I went there far from convinced that this transatlantic technique would prove desirable if introduced to our schools, but found so much profound good sense and such complete lack of prejudice in those concerned with the course, that I made a further three visits and persuaded Professor Wrenn to come to Chelmsford to address the county Inspectors, Organisers and psychologists. One result of his visit was that Mr. White, Chief Inspector for Essex, and I agreed that a local experiment was certainly desirable. Why 'experiment'? Because had we suggested that counselling be generally introduced we might well have met a flat refusal. Nor indeed did we then feel able to produce hard evidence that a counselling service would be a more profitable investment of public money than other calls on the L.E.A. purse, judged from the point of view of child benefit. What we had was a kind of hunch: counselling—yes; whether by counsellors was yet to be proved.

We have now had a year in which three fully trained counsellors have been working. One has been appointed on Scale 'D', two on 'C', and all in comprehensive schools of 900 or more. Although Mr. White and I were told that we could have an experiment involving four counsellors up to Scale 'D' at the final stage of all the arrangements necessarily involved, the Committee concerned approved the experiment 'provided it does not cost us any money'. This meant in effect that instead of the four posts being in addition to establishment we could now effect their introduction only by persuading headteachers of comprehensive schools that they should allocate one of their posts for this purpose. In our discussions with certain of the headteachers in Essex it became clear to us that the large majority of the most able heads in Essex had already made provision for improved pastoral care of their children by means of house tutors. The result has been that we have three of the four posts filled and although several more Essex heads now want counsellors, they want them if appointed above the establishment.

The current Essex school population is 181,782 and since the Essex Education Committee follows the Underwood Report's recommended proportions there is a current establishment for 17 psychologists, of which some 14 are in post, plus several other psychologists employed on a sessional basis. When a psychologist is first appointed to work with Essex, I do not tell him how to carry out his job. It is far too young a profession for it to be anything other than arrogant for anyone to claim that his methods are definitive. Therefore, a wide range of professional practices reflecting individual abilities and predilections exists within the modulating framework of the clinic and the School Psychological Service.

If educational psychology is regarded as having most of its growing yet to do, surely this is *a fortiori* true of counselling. It seems to me that the first five years of counselling practice will establish a series of templates partly determined by the scope afforded counsellors by their local education authorities which may well shape their successors' practice in years to come. But since it is already being said that it is impossible to train a teacher to play all the rôles of personal, educational and vocational counselling completely adequately in one year, perhaps the establishment of a body of accepted practice in counselling is further away than five years.

Four years ago I was asked by the County Youth Employment Officer if I could help in bringing about an increase in objectivity in the assessments of children with whom her Careers Advisory Officers were concerned, by training quite a large number of her staff in the administration of the General Aptitude Test Battery (Morrisby) and the Rothwell-Miller Vocational Interest Blank, and in the rudimentary interpretation of these. Certain very useful results have resulted during the last four years when 1,000 boys and girls at the end of their fourth year in the secondary selective course have been tested in urban, rural, mixed, single-sex, comprehensive, bi-lateral and grammar schools. It seems likely that the very existence of this 'between schools' yardstick is responsible for the (generally reported) significant improvement in the quality of the schools' reports about the individual child; and the Careers Advisory Officers unanimously report that their interviews involve the child much more as a result of the use of the Rothwell-Miller Vocational Interest Blank.

It is perhaps relevant to point out that secondary headteachers throughout Essex have now formally asked that some similar programme of testing be made available to all of them. Now whatever the merits of the Morrisby test one thing seems clear to me. The fact that people other than psychologists sought the use of psychometric testing was a clear warning that if they did not receive the help of the school Psychological Service they would go elsewhere. Testing would have resulted with probably lower validity than is now the case. Thus the results that have been achieved could not have been achieved by the combined efforts of all the Essex psychologists. We have neither the time to devote ourselves exclusively to this aspect of our work, which is properly a call on our time, nor have we the opportunities. Moral; accept help when it is offered—but sign nothing without reading the small print.

In large schools, those with say over 1,000, the newly appointed counsellor has to establish his own order of priorities—to spread himself thinly or to decide where he can make his contribution most valuably. Daws (1967) suggests that this might take the form of 'therapeutic counselling':

The therapeutic counsellor would concern himself only with those children and young people who show evidence of stress and disturbance: the persistently truanting child, the overly aggressive child, the silent withdrawn child, the delinquent, the bereaved, the 'new boy', the under-achiever, the sexual offender, the rejected child and the child disturbed at the prospect of examinations. There would be no shortage of clients, but as they will be a relatively small proportion of the total school population at any one time, and as he will refer the more serious cases elsewhere, his caseload should allow him to devote more time to each child than would be available to a personal counsellor.

His first task when a child is brought to his notice would be to exercise his diagnostic skill in discriminating what is essentially healthy disturbance—a normal reaction to a situation of stress—from that which betrays underlying morbidity, perhaps due to long-standing exposure to a high level of stress. The disturbed child will become his client; the severely disturbed child he will refer with a report to the school psychological service who in turn can make use of the guidance clinic or the child psychiatry unit (B.P.S. 1962). He may also expect some diagnostic help from the visiting school medical officer, and from the school psychological service, where one exists. Such a rôle would ensure that seriously disturbed children are identified and referred for specialist attention earlier than usual and that many who would ultimately have deteriorated to a level necessitating psychiatric attention will be identified in good time and helped to cope with their difficulties and to survive them without damage. Such a therapeutic rôle would involve the counsellor's working with the parents no less than the child to help them play a significant part in the therapeutic process, and with such home-directed counselling he will find a valuable ally in the school social worker if the school is fortunate enough to have one. (*Op. cit.*, p. 89.)

As far as diagnosis by the counsellor and referrals to the clinic are concerned, the present situation in Essex is that I ask head-teachers to refer to the psychologists any child about whom they have some doubt, or who is making his need for help more manifest. Prevention, I think, is the best therapy. If the psychologist is found to be useful by the school it is the readier to refer. Therefore a waiting list is to be expected. If this becomes of the order of more than a month (and in some parts of the country more than six months is common), schools may well be reluctant to refer, because by the time something happens the problem may have resolved itself or will at least be different. One means of alleviating this difficulty is for the psychologist to keep one half-day a week clear of any form of commitment to clinic or school psychological service waiting list, and to inform their schools of this so that they know that the educational psychologist is available to see emergencies or other urgent cases on Thursday afternoon, for example. I have further asked my colleagues that if Thursday afternoon arrives without their having received any emergency calls, they should not take the next few cases from the waiting lists but should go into the schools and drink tea, because I believe that schools still contain many teachers who regard psychologists as those relatively queer people who deal with relatively queer children, and who will refer children to the psychologist only when they have exhausted their repertoire of teaching techniques and in a sense these referrals become regarded as an admission of failure.

We are indebted to Mr. C. J. Gill for his proposed definition of a school counsellor:

> To his teaching colleagues, he is a specialist to whom they may send their problem children. To the specialist referral agencies, however, he is a general practitioner whose purpose is to refer to them those children who need their specialist attention. That is, he is to serve his teacher colleagues and the ancillary services no less than his clients. (Quoted in Daws, 1967.)

Reverting to the current system in which heads are encouraged to refer children to the psychologist readily, surely the interposition of a trained counsellor acting as a filter can only release the psychologist to do more of the sort of work he, not the counsellor, can do. But this needs mutual confidence. So the first responsibility of the psychologist when a counsellor is appointed is to go to the school and encourage him to feel 'part of the team' with regard to the clinic and School Psychological Service. The psychologist should then attempt to facilitate the acceptance of the counsellor by the psychiatrist at the clinic. It should not be assumed by the psychologist that the psychiatrist will be informed about the counsellor's rôle and training, and diplomatic courses (called 'conferences') of an in-service training nature should then be arranged by the psychologist or his boss. These would be aimed at psychiatrists and certain heads. Later courses should be arranged for teachers.

Now at this point I want to quote from a report prepared by one of my colleagues and written without my prior knowledge. It is a résumé of the points covered in a discussion at a meeting arranged by him with three counsellors in Essex. The report is entitled *Counselling and the Child Guidance and School Psychological Services*.

> The most important function of the counsellor is to act as a link between the school and the School Psychological Service and Child

Guidance Service. The trained counsellor possesses an understanding of the rôle of these services, and should be able to decide how far they can help individual children. Thus the task of the counsellor in relation to both these services is to pass on to them such cases as he believes appropriate for them to deal with. The counsellor, either by his initial screening processes, or by referrals to him either spontaneously or from other teachers, becomes aware of the problem children within his school. He has been trained to deal with many of these problems by bringing the children to deal with their difficulties themselves, and adjusting their reactions to them or by other means. In the majority of cases, therefore, there will be no need to refer the cases to an outside agency. However, in some cases he may either need advice on how to proceed with a child, or the direct help of one of the agencies.

In practice, the school counsellor in Brentwood has collaborated with the educational psychologists to attempt to solve some of the more difficult problems encountered among the pupils in the school. In particular such problems as school phobia are more speedily and effectively dealt with than has been the case in the past. There is an immediacy and flexibility about this approach to personal problems— using staff within the school, yet drawing on the help of an outside service.

For the counsellor to become a very effective link between school and the Child Guidance Service, it is necessary for this service to realise the functions of the counsellor. It is not uncommon for psychiatrists to know nothing about counselling, and it seems that until they are aware of the value of this service, they will fail to take advantage of the supportive therapy that might be offered Child Guidance patients. Counsellors should be involved much more in the work of the Child Guidance Service, and their attendance at case conferences is desirable. So far, in Brentwood, the counsellor has been asked to attend conferences where the Children's Department and the Probation Service have been represented. At such conferences he is able to speak with greater knowledge and certainty about individual cases than any other teacher in the school, and as such, not only informs the other agencies of the child's standing at school, but can also carry back to the school the suggestions and recommendations made by these agencies.

The dual rôle of the counsellor, therefore, as both initiator of referrals and as an external member of the Child Guidance Service giving supportive therapy, is one which is emerging at present, though in order for these functions to be given full clarity, much more understanding and assistance is required from the Child Guidance Service.

My colleague, Mr. Cornwall, is perfectly correct to highlight the need for action by myself and the other psychologists in

Essex as well as by those responsible for the in-service training programme of teachers.

Because the psychologist will probably be the most informed of the ancillary officers available to the school the counsellor may come to turn to him more than to any of the other services. It has already been suggested that school counsellors should be paid on Soulbury Scale I, that is the same scale (at a lower rate) as psychologists. I have strongly opposed this suggestion as it would seem to me to prejudice strongly the acceptance by teachers of the fact that the counsellor is a member of the school staff, that he is to act as liaison between the school and child. If he were thus to be seen to be explicitly linked to one of these ancillary services it might well prejudice the development and liaison with the other ancillary services available to the school. It has been said that the counsellor is at risk of becoming a 'mini-psychologist'. This is nonsense. He has probably taught a great deal longer than the psychologist and his rôle is complementary and not that of a competitor.

The counsellor's rôle *vis-à-vis* the clinics will be modulated by the psychiatrist's persuasion. If he is very Freudian he may throw up his hands and mutter 'but psychology is a complex business' when it is suggested that counsellors play a supportive rôle in certain selected cases. This despite the fact that he is probably seeing fewer children than most. If the psychiatrist is eclectic, he will see more children and may be prepared to accept that kind of help which the counsellor could give. Providing the psychologist has confidence in the counsellor's capacity to handle the supportive rôle with certain selected cases, he may well re-refer to the counsellor children originally referred to him by the counsellor—and by this co-operation based on mutual respect and trust more may get done.

Recently, I learnt of one means by which a counsellor has achieved acceptance by the other members of staff of the girls' school in which she currently works. She administered the High School Personality Questionnaire to half of the girls in the fourth year and this procedure highlighted thirty cases of girls who needed help in various degrees. Eight of these cases were under such stress that it has required much work by the coun-sellor and with their homes. The point to be stressed here, I think, is that despite the genuinely held belief by the other teachers who had had responsibility for this year group, that they knew their children, none of these thirty girls had previously been thought to be under stress; but the manifest improvement in their demeanour after receiving the counsellor's help had been a tangible proof in the eyes of several of the staff concerned that the counsellor has a real contribution to make, which is not in competition with their own.

Perhaps at this point it would be helpful to offer one or two observations concerning points of difficulty which arise when it is suggested that a counsellor be introduced to a school. First and foremost it is certainly true that the head must be persuaded of the advantage to the school of having a counsellor on his staff; but since these counsellors, in Essex at least, are not supernumerary this can be taken for granted. It is very helpful if efforts are made to win over all, or most, of the staff toward the idea of a counsellor—but if counsellors are to be placed (as those in charge of the Keele course suggest) at about number three in a large secondary school, and if they do not teach, then indeed the other members of the staff must be completely persuaded if no resentments are to be aroused.

In the event, we have not found any school where no resentments or anxieties have been created. The member of staff to feel most threatened by the suggestion to introduce a counsellor has been the careers teacher, and it is a signal comment on the effectiveness of one of the counsellors mentioned above that the careers mistress in the school concerned has actively campaigned for her acceptance by other, and new, members of staff. One can quite understand how resentments would be occasioned if this relatively highly paid teacher does not teach, especially if influenza empties classrooms. As it happens, in each of the Essex schools concerned the counsellor has taught for some fraction of his or her time. There may indeed be some advantage in the counsellor teaching a disappearing fraction of the school population (for example, sixth form pupils who will disappear from the school) since this will show those of the counsellor's colleagues who are not as yet fully convinced that she can in fact teach.

It has been suggested that counsellors should always teach some proportion of their week, and the main argument against this seems to be that American experience tends to suggest that the rôles of teacher and counsellor cannot be reconciled without prejudice to one of them. In other words, if a counsellor teaches a child he is, to some extent at least, seen as a figure of authority, and it is by no means certain that this perception of the

60

counsellor may not inhibit the child when he subsequently visits the counsellor. My own view is that given the right sort of warm personality the counsellor could teach a child and despite this receive his or her confidences in the interview situation. I very much doubt, however, whether a child having been taught by the counsellor, and despite being prepared to offer confidences, would indeed be prepared to disclose intimacies to the counsellor, and these may be of crucial importance. Such practice as we have been able to observe in Essex, moreover, makes it clear that once the staff have accepted the counsellor, as such, then they refer children increasingly frequently, and the rate of self-referral by the children has, in each of the schools concerned, risen steadily throughout the year. Indeed, the headmaster of one of the schools concerned, with one counsellor on Scale 'D', has stated that he felt he could benefit from the services of another counsellor.

One of the aspects of counselling procedure in the United States, as reported in the literature, that occasioned me some doubt about the suitability of introducing counselling as practised in America into our schools was the wide use made of non-directive interview techniques as derived from Carl Rogers' psycho-therapeutic practice. Woody (1968) advocates a system of 'behavioural counselling' for use in British schools. In this rôle the counsellor would reinforce certain aspects of the child's conversation and indeed make suggestions where appropriate in order to help resolve the difficulty of the moment. Dr. Lytton puts this very well when he describes this as an increase of focussing by the counsellor, and something of this nature has probably already characterised much counselling practice in this country. No doubt this is an inevitable result of the fact that all counsellors in British schools have far more children than they can possibly help adequately. As was stated above, I think it inevitable that counsellors in English schools will decide where they can make their best contribution in the light of their own abilities and predilections and in the circumstances of the particular school.

Perhaps, therefore, the most important rôle that the psychologist can play in these early years of counselling is to provide a sympathetic professional ear to a colleague in need of it; to listen, to make constructive suggestions, and to facilitate via his administrative colleagues developments that seem desirable to both. Once this relationship has been established by the counsellor and the psychologist, many important opportunities become available. It is, presumably, not in dispute that educational psychologists have insufficient time to carry out that quality of liaison with the school concerning individual cases that they would wish. We all overwork and if, therefore, we can have confidence in a specially trained, insightful, and sympathetic counsellor in a school, how much better can we mediate the total welfare of a clinic case by using the counsellor in the school concerned. And the feedback is important, this traffic can be two-way.

Recently, for example, the mother of a girl attending the Child Guidance Clinic came to a counsellor asking for help. 'But I thought you had been to see Dr. X?' (the psychiatrist). 'Yes, but I have come to you for help (it's my psychiatrist you see, he doesn't understand me).' By virtue of the counsellor's liaison with the psychologist the difficulties that this particular mother was experiencing were rapidly and easily resolved. Again, given that the psychologist feels confidence in the quality of the counsellor—and this I believe is arrived at very often by experienced psychologists and psychiatrists as 'a feeling in the pit of one's stomach'—the situation can arise where the psychologist can re-refer to the counsellor a child originally referred to him by the counsellor, because once he has applied those particular skills which he alone possesses he can, by working with and through the counsellor, achieve the most desirable result for the child.

The counsellor is not to be regarded as explicitly a part of the Child Guidance or School Psychological Services—this is undesirable—but by ensuring that first our clinical colleagues become informed and persuaded of the counsellor's contribution, and then if our colleagues in the other non-teaching ancillary services do too, we may indeed achieve a situation in which the counsellor not only does good—but is seen to do good.

6. The School Counsellor and the Youth Employment Service

Catherine Avent

While this paper is entitled 'The School Counsellor and the Youth Employment Service' I prefer to think in terms of 'careers advisers', though well aware of the fact that at the present time, officers of Local Education Authority Youth Employment Services are variously called 'Youth Employment Officer', 'Careers Officer', 'Careers Advisory Officer', 'Careers Adviser' and 'Vocational Guidance Officer'. I think it is important that we should get away from the idea of a person primarily concerned with helping boys and girls (mainly leaving at the age of fifteen or sixteen) to get jobs; this is the image conjured up by the original title 'Youth Employment Officer'. So I shall refer to careers advisers, but by that I mean, not the careers master or mistress of a school, but the officer employed mainly by the Local Education Authority (or in a few areas the Ministry of Labour), to provide a service of careers advice, placing in employment and follow-up of young workers.

It could be said that the term 'school counsellor' is also badly in need of definition, and it may be worth considering Dr. James Conant's comment on the rôle of the counsellor, as set out in his book *The Comprehensive High School* (1967):

> In a satisfactory school system the counseling should start in the elementary school, and there should be good articulation between the counseling in the junior and senior high schools. . . . There should be one full-time counselor or guidance officer for every 250–300 pupils in the high school. The counselors should have had experience as teachers, but should be devoting virtually full time to the counseling work; they should be familiar with the use of tests and measurements of the aptitudes and achievement of pupils. The function of the counselor is not to supplant the parents but to supplement parental advice to a youngster. To this end, the counselor should be in close

63

touch with the parent as well as the pupil. Through consultation, an attempt should be made each year to work out an elective program for the student which corresponds to the student's interest and ability as determined by tests of scholastic aptitude, the recorded achievement as measured by grades in courses and by teachers' estimates. The counselors should be sympathetic to the elective programs which develop marketable skills; they should also understand the program for the slow readers and be ready to co-operate with the teachers of this group of students. (Conant, 1967.)

If we take it as axiomatic that the counsellor is involved in three main functions, personal, educational and vocational counselling, it may help us to see the relationship between the counsellor and the careers adviser. In the United States, counsellors are mainly concerned in the educational and personal counselling of students in the high school; this is because the boy or girl in an American high school is not normally required to make vocational choices as early as pupils in this country. Most careers advisers here accept the desirability of what Professor Alec Rodger has called 'planned procrastination' in that it is clearly desirable for pupils to have as long as possible a general education, and to postpone irrevocable decisions on career choice or educational choices which to a great extent determine the careers available. Vocational guidance is therefore very much more required in British schools than in American schools where the majority of students (as many as 85 per cent in most schools) are expecting to remain in full-time education until the age of eighteen, and of whom many will then proceed to liberal arts colleges pursuing a higher education which is not specifically related to any particular profession.

The American counsellor is required to undertake advice to pupils on the vast range of subjects available in the curriculum. In Britain we have traditionally provided what I might term a *table d'hôte* menu varying only in that, while boys have taken woodwork and metalwork, the girls have done cookery and needlework, and an *à la carte* menu for the sixth formers who have been able to choose between science courses, arts courses and perhaps a general or economic sixth. But in our comprehensive schools we are now providing something approaching the 'cafeteria' system available in an American high school. I know of one metropolitan school where the headmaster claims to provide more than three hundred and fifty different permutations of the subjects available within the school. It is clear that in such a system, pupils need help in making subject choices which will not only provide a good general education, but enable them to go on thereafter to any appropriate tertiary education or industrial training.

The tradition of personal counselling, which has been in operation for more than fifty years in the United States, has only recently been introduced into British schools and is still perhaps thought of as a fringe activity mainly required by pupils with specific problems related to their learning adjustment or home circumstances. The counsellor in a British school, therefore, crosses the path of the careers adviser in two distinct ways: he is likely to be the link in providing information of a personal nature on the students' circumstances, interests, personality and problems. But he may also be the person on the school's staff most concerned in helping pupils to make educational and vocational decisions and this, of course, means that his work is tangential to the work of the careers adviser coming into the school with knowledge of the requirements of occupations and the appropriate education and training for them.

If we may first think of the counsellor mainly concerned with personal counselling. I would expect that he would be able to identify those pupils who have special needs and circumstances, which the careers adviser should be aware of when giving educational and vocational guidance. He is the person most likely to know whether it is in a pupil's interests that he should obtain training or employment away from home because of domestic circumstances; he is likely to know whether it is the considered opinion of other members of the school's staff that this pupil finds difficulty in studying on his own or needs to be in a situation where he will be closely supervised. This kind of liaison work is very obvious.

I would like to consider in more detail the relationship of the school counsellor with the careers adviser in those cases where the counsellor is undertaking a measure of educational and vocational counselling within the school. Perhaps it would be useful to consider an ideal situation in which the counsellor has an office suitably equipped for private interviews, and facilities for the storage and distribution of information on further education and careers. Let us suppose that the counsellor is a person of considerable status within the school and can act as the tutor/organiser of the educational and careers guidance programme. It is likely that the counsellor (if on a full-time basis) might be given responsibility for careers information on the grounds that he is available in an office, not having to keep his files in a classroom; that he is not in any particular disciplinary relationship with any of the pupils; nor the teacher of a possibly hated or despised subject. If he is responsible for information storage and retrieval one would expect him to have adequate filing cabinets, cupboards and a display space, perhaps comparable to a small shop window on the scale, for example, of a tuck shop. Careers information in many schools has traditionally been kept on the principle either of the chained Bible, only available on request from a locked drawer in the headmaster's desk, or, alternatively, as was described by one careers mistress, on 'the bin system'—where the girls had to scrabble in a large bin into which all careers pamphlets had been thrown!

If the counsellor is the tutor/organiser for careers with a head of department status, I would expect moreover that he would be able to overcome some of the rivalry that sometimes takes place within the staff-room when discussions are held about the university or college destination of some of the academically able pupils.

Clearly, if the counsellor is a person of status within the school and is undertaking responsibility for careers work, there is a good case for a team approach; at present a great deal of time is wasted by careers advisers and specialists introduced into schools who may find themselves giving the same information to a succession of individuals or small groups. A system whereby large groups receive basic information or see films and listen to television and sound broadcasts, while members of staff and of the Youth Employment Service are available to follow up these general activities with small groups or a few interested pupils, can obviously be more effective.

Counsellors will have had some initial training in psychological techniques and are therefore in a good position to introduce a programme of tests to determine aptitudes and abilities which may not have been shown up during the normal school course. Much more effective careers advice will probably be given to pupils who have had the opportunity of undergoing some limited test programme of this sort. If there is no money available for this, then at least it may be possible for the counsellor to administer interest inventories so that the pupils have more opportunity to consider their vocational interests and even perhaps to discuss within a group each other's interests, as shown on the scores in these inventories. It is clearly easier to do this kind of group counselling as a result of interest inventories, since there is no question of value judgements being made as might appear if groups discussed each other's test results in connection with such things as mechanical aptitude, spatial perception, and so forth.

Obviously, one of the main advantages to the Youth Employment Service in the appointment of a counsellor to a school should be that the pupils will have been much better prepared for their vocational guidance interviews. One assumes that at each stage the counsellor will be able to interview the pupil before he sees the careers adviser. If the counsellor is responsible for the organisation of the careers programme within the school it will be necessary for him to work out a system, within the time available, which will ensure that he is available for any pupil who has a problem and wishes to consult him; while at the same time, he conducts some regular-contact sessions with each pupil in order to avoid the risk of some who may in fact need counselling never declaring themselves by self-referral to the counsellor. An ideal careers programme ought probably to start in the third year of the secondary course, or at any rate before educational decisions are made which have vocational consequences. The optimum is probably for each pupil throughout his school years, from the third to the upper sixth form, to have at least one period a week which has a careers content, even if it is not in fact labelled careers but is part of the English course or vocational studies, or whatever seems appropriate.

The counsellor is likely to be the person most in touch with parents, and one hopes that he will be able to involve parents much more than has hitherto happened in the stages of decision-making which upper school pupils undergo. Parents have been variously described as the 'negative', who do not come near the school, and who appear to give no encouragement to the pupil or even appear to blame him for wanting to remain at school beyond the minimum age or the age at which they themselves left; the 'passive', who take the line that they only want their child to be happy and will not use any influence on him; and the 'positive', who may be projecting their own thwarted ambitions on to their children, and may be unable to understand why a girl prefers to work in a store or be a hairdresser rather than become a shorthand-typist or something apparently more socially desirable to her mother. I have always felt that we do not make enough use of parental knowledge and expertise, and I would like to see parents used in a much more constructive way in the process of careers guidance. A keen counsellor would perhaps be able to enlist the enthusiasm of parents who could be in many cases more useful than the representatives of local professional people, rotarians and other adults who are at present invited to take part in careers conventions—provided, of course, that it was clearly established that professional careers advice would be given by the professional adviser, and that the parent was not expected to be in a position to advise on various methods of training but rather to describe the actual work he does.

The careers adviser from the Youth Employment Service does not normally undertake home visiting, so that in cases where this was desirable it would presumably be undertaken by the counsellor; nor is he equipped as a personal problem-solver or helper in difficulties of learning adjustment. He is, however, in a better position than the counsellor to be the liaison between the school and the further educational institutions and the world of work. Careers can be used to motivate pupils to higher achievement, and more might be done in schools where there was a counsellor to involve the pupils themselves in their careers programme. The careers adviser has his own problem youngsters: the job-changers, the homeless, the unemployed, the pregnant, the handicapped, the delinquent, the seekers after high wages, the immigrants, and the first generation in a family to have an academic education leading to university. These and many others present him with his own type of social work problem and challenge. One of the ways in which the careers adviser and the counsellor can work most effectively together will be, not only in the team co-ordinating the careers work of the school, but perhaps in using past pupils of a school in order to help the next generation. A follow-up, undertaken by the counsellor not just for his own records, but to improve the knowledge of present pupils about the destination of those who left in previous years, might well lead to the use of young people in their twenties as consultants rather than officials of professional organisations.

Some sort of market research whereby pupils were asked to write essays on the kinds of people they would like to meet, or occupations they would like to see, could be followed by critiques of broadcasts, films, visits, speakers, and so forth, conducted in the normal English syllabus. All this kind of activity could be admirably co-ordinated by the counsellor. Many people think some careers advisers are undertaking far too many sessions in school where they are actually giving talks on occupations. It seems to me that it is not the task of the careers adviser to be taking regular weekly classes, but rather of the *careers tutor* and if this person is also the counsellor the task would be much easier. In the same way, I personally doubt the value of the so-called 'clinic' whereby a careers adviser is available in a school, say, every Tuesday afternoon, in case any pupils wish to see him for information. Not only does this mean that he may be over-lapping with the work of the counsellor, but there is the danger that pupils ask him for information on the requirements of occupations and then go away and say they have been *advised* to enter that occupation.

I would like to say quite emphatically that I do not consider it is the counsellor's job or the careers tutor's to *place young people in employment,* that is to say, to give them actual intro-ductions to employers known to have vacancies. Not only does this deny both pupil and employer the maximum choice, but it prevents the employer from feeling that he has one intermediary to whom to notify his vacancy and from whom to get selected applicants.

Some young people are determined to leave school at fifteen or sixteen and do so with the agreement of their parents and the approval of their teachers. These agreed leavers should in my view be referred to the careers adviser. It is, furthermore, the careers adviser's job to organise any works-experience schemes, because he is likely to have better knowledge than any person on the staff of one school can have of the organisations which offer the best training and therefore the best view to intending entrants. If the school has an Open Day I would hope that the careers tutor would be able to organise exhibitions of occupations which are related to each of the major subjects on the school timetable. In this way he will get the co-operation of the teachers of non-vocational subjects, and be instrumental in encouraging pupils gifted in languages and the humanities who sometimes feel that in a philistine world their particular abilities will have no marketable value.

Clearly, no careers adviser can know the boys and girls as well as the counsellor. The careers adviser, on the other hand, should be more objective. Perhaps one definition might be that the careers adviser is more *directive* in his approach to pupils, while the counsellor is more *non-directive*. If the Youth Employment Service is to be organised in larger units in the future as a result of local government reorganisation, there is likely to be more specialisation, as applies at the moment with those with special responsibilities for sixth formers or for the handicapped. There will be even more need, therefore, for counsellors to co-ordinate the activities of a larger team of people coming to the school to work with the pupils in their careers guidance activities. There is every case for emphasising that this is a *team activity*, helping pupils towards what is necessarily an uncertain future. Perhaps I might end with a quotation from the posters in the New York subway:

'Ha! Ha! Think school's a laugh? You won't think it so funny when you can't get a good paying job. To get a good paying job get a good education.'

A Comment on Part Three

John Cowie

The school counsellor and the child guidance clinic

Child and adolescent psychiatry has evolved out of a cluster of such pragmatic and academic activities as child welfare, care of the mentally subnormal, education, developmental psychology, psychoanalysis, Pavlovian theory, child guidance clinics, sociology, learning theory and community care programmes.

The last few decades have seen a revolution in psychiatry. New psychopharmacological drugs in the mid-1950's and basic research in neuro-chemistry, neuro-physiology and neuro-pharmacology have opened up vast new perspectives. In recent years, it has been discovered that anomalies of the sex chromosomes are often associated with severe personality and character disorders, severe violence, crime and delinquency. Behaviour patterns of this kind have been observed in children in association with sex chromosomal aberrations and brain wave rhythm changes are often recorded (Cowie and Kahn, 1968). A new breed of child psychiatrists is emerging who are trained to diagnose and possibly treat organic factors that may underly abnormal behaviour patterns.

However, many child guidance teams are still entrenched behind the notion that all aberrant behaviour is primarily emotionally determined and therefore must yield, given time, to psychotherapy and intensive casework. For some years there has been an increasing number of workers who question the efficacy of psychotherapeutic magic. William Schofield, Professor of Psychiatry at the University of Minnesota, in his book, *Psychotherapy: the Purchase of Friendship* (1964), critically examines some of the hypotheses underlying the mystique of psychotherapy. He concludes that what most patients are seeking is a

71

kind of friendship with the therapist, and the lonely, frustrated, anxious, depressed or deprived child may have a similar intent with the counsellor. The therapeutic counsellor may call this need and the satisfying of it, neurosis and psychotherapy. In talking to his client the counsellor is helping and befriending him and such conversation is a dialectic exercise with a therapeutic effect. 'Therapeutic conversation' is possibly a more apt description of this process than psychotherapy and all that this title implies.

The counsellor may assume that the professional therapist in the clinic team must have a body of firmly established knowledge which permits him to act with confidence and efficacy in the treatment of disturbed children. In reality, there has been minimal scientific research in this area and although what therapists do may be effective, it must be accepted that this is based on lore rather than scientific knowledge. The counsellor must base a decision to call in ancillary help as much on practical common-sense grounds as on any professional know-how.

Mr. Robb advises the counsellor to find out the psychiatrist's particular persuasion. This is often a hopeless task, largely because psychiatrists who have had a training in psychoanalysis do not communicate this knowledge readily and the so-called eclectic is often a poorly trained psychiatrist who has dabbled in many fields. Mr. Robb and other speakers have stressed the need to select the right person for the job of counselling. The counsellor should try to come to terms with the clinic team as individuals and sort out those members of the team whose personalities would fit most closely the needs of their clients, whether acting individually or in concert with the counsellor. For clinical diagnosis the psychiatrist is the most appropriate person in the team.

There is a growing awareness that the processes involved in learning and the development of the personality are intimately related. Abnormality in one may cause an imbalance that abnormally affects the other. For example, there is some evidence that there is a significant relationship between reading retardation and psychopathy (Cowie *et al.*, 1968). The under-achieving, socially underprivileged child may have more anxieties connected with school than the child from a reasonable home. He sees at first hand the price of lack of success, and sometimes his parents who are failures themselves, project just as high academic expectations as parents who themselves have been academically successful, but who, at least, provide a standard by example. The child who can function normally at school almost certainly makes a successful adult, whereas the severity and chronicity of behaviour disturbance in children has been found to correlate highly with breakdown in later life. Teachers who can spot intuitively or by training and experience the early signs of disturbance and can alert the appropriate experts, are providing an invaluable service to the child in need.

The educational psychologist is the link between school and clinic because the psychologist has a mandate to function directly in schools. All problems should be fully discussed by the counsellor with all personnel concerned before putting the administrative procedures involved in clinic referral into operation. Child Guidance Clinics have a poor reputation for alleviating the psychological ills of deprived children living in a materially and emotionally starved home environment. These children and their parents do not easily accept the abstract reasoning and the bother of repeated attendance that classical child psychiatric clinics demand. The counsellor must be prepared to learn from experience the kind of problem and kind of child most likely to benefit from the clinic. The clinic team should be prepared at all times to go into the school and, from within the school milieu, can act as skilled observers and advisers. They may then select pupils for further investigations at the clinic if necessary. The average pupil spends five hours a day for three terms a year in school, and altogether may spend around eleven thousand hours of his life there. This allows time for an immense number of potentially therapeutic encounters between pupil and involved adult. Within the school environment naturally occurring behaviour patterns can be observed and their development noted, channelled, blocked, modified or eliminated. Counsellors acting individually or in concert with ancillary experts can do much to detect pathological group behaviour patterns and can play a direct or a linking rôle as the occasion demands.

Sometimes disturbed children are withdrawn from their normal schooling for part of the day into special classes where the teachers use techniques that are essentially a combination of behaviour therapy and re-education by operant conditioning. In this type of situation the counsellor plays an important rôle as co-therapist, whilst the clinic plays an overall observing and reassessing rôle.

There is some controversy about whether or not a counsellor

should act as a teacher as well. Mr. Robb avoids this issue. In my view a counsellor may lose something of therapeutic value if he rationalises his way out of a teaching rôle. If he is open to inspection by all pupils, future clients can measure his worth as a teacher and make up their minds about consulting the counsellor based on this intuitive like or dislike. The least successful teacher also appears to make the least successful counsellor—a man no one likes to consult.

Finally, Mr. Robb exhorts his psychologists to go into schools, make contact, and drink tea. I would recommend counsellors to go into clinics and drink what is offered by the clinic secretary and then reciprocate the hospitality. It is of vital importance that the counsellor should appraise the services available and acquire an up-to-date knowledge of what modern child psychiatry can offer.

The school counsellor and the youth employment service

All societies preceding ours defined the goals and aspirations of their members. These were often limited and localised to class and caste. Modern western civilisation eliminates specific goals and aspirations, and firm demarcations of caste and class structures are dropped. Control of aspirations is released and every individual is allowed to strive and aspire towards any chosen goal. Our society is dominated by technology, and economic survival is dependent on the acquisition of specialised knowledge by a proportion of its members. Selection for training for specialist rôles is demanded by society, hence the need for a trained adult to give guidance in this area.

In order to motivate the child to study, implications are made that there are no upper limits and the highest goals can be reached. The third most common question put to a child (after name and age) by interested adults is: 'What are you going to be when you grow up?' Depending on the age of the child, the answer is either an unrealistic one based on fantasy, or a declaration of intention to follow one or other parent's footsteps. Parental ambitions and hopes for the future of their children are instilled early and reinforced by society. Children's omnipotent fantasies are supported by fond parents who see in them future Prime Ministers, Nobel Prize winners, or in a Bessie Bunter type, a prima donna performing at Covent Garden. Any policeman can become a Sherlock Holmes, and a marshal's baton is said to be in every soldier's knapsack!

With advancing computer-controlled automation, opportunities for fulfilling hopes of work satisfaction recede as competition increases and the standards required rise. Increasing numbers of reasonably gifted school leavers become disappointed, disenchanted, frustrated and resentful, and the more susceptible of them may break down or show personality and character deviations. They may seek to satisfy their fantasied needs legally through gambling (pools, bingo and State Lotteries are the current vogue), or illegally through crime and delinquency. Others give up the struggle and retreat from reality with the aid of drugs, drink, sex, or in joining in 'off-beat' group activities. In the school environment many warning signals are apparent to the experienced teacher at a fairly early stage, and counsellors and careers masters look for these hints in previous reports.

Miss Avent in her paper strictly destroys the notion that the Youth Employment Officer is a job getter, or an expert at finding jobs that carry the most perquisites or give an opportunity for the greatest 'fiddle'. She substitutes the title 'Careers Adviser' for 'Youth Employment Officer'. She constantly emphasises the paramount rôle of the professional adviser as an expert who is able to give a pupil insight into actual and potential capacities and enlighten them on the motivations and fantasies underlying their careers' needs. The Careers Adviser's objective evaluations of potentialities can then be equated realistically with work opportunities in any particular geographical area.

More gifted pupils select themselves for higher education opportunities, but in this country entrance to the older established universities is becoming increasingly difficult as the number of suitable entrants rises and a system of priorities operates. The need for skilled, sophisticated advice is probably greater for this particular group than for the less gifted whose very dullness may itself act as an opiate against the frustration of failure to fulfil personal or parent-induced aspirations. In the U.S.A. this need for a higher education is recognised and met. In this country we appear to be moving towards total comprehensive education, and its corollary might be different levels of university education similar to practice in the U.S.A. of which country Miss Avent has had considerable practical experience.

In our present economic state it may be many decades before we can afford separate specialists functioning in the separate rôles of counsellor and careers adviser. The person skilled in the art of co-ordinating the efforts of relevant personnel in the ancillary services, and in formulating the problems of individual pupils from their own observations and from data obtained from others in the school service, might be of more value than several experts who each might interpret differently emotional factors and underlying motivations.

PART FOUR   PERSPECTIVES ON COUNSELLING

7. An Integrated Approach to Counselling and Social Work—A look into the future

Hugh Lytton

America has been mentioned repeatedly in this symposium. So far as counselling is concerned, which comes to us across the Atlantic, we are in a love-hate relationship with that country and we have to find a rational way of differentiating ourselves from it. I will therefore take as my beginning text Lord Bowden's magnificent generalisation:

> In the past Britain's educational system has tended to model itself on that of the U.S.A.—with a time-lag which happens usually to be about 30 years (Bowden, 1968).

An over-simplification, perhaps, and we may, of course, deplore it, but before rushing in with our protest we should remember the saga of a Mr. Priest, a Post Office official. This gentleman informed a parliamentary committee in 1875, speaking of the telephone, that there was no call for this new-fangled American device in Britain because we had plenty of excellent messenger boys here. Years later, the same Priest assured another committee that U.S. automatic telephone exchanges were redundant in the U.K. because of our large pool of low-paid girl telephonists . . . The only other thing we know about Mr. Priest is that when he died in 1912, his obituary called him 'the father of the British telephone system'.

This cautionary tale illustrates some of the less rational difficulties inherent in the transplantation even of mechanical devices from one culture to another, difficulties that are nevertheless real enough from a psychological point of view. There are also some more rational and real impediments in the way of such a transplantation, how much more so when it is a question of a social institution, rather than a mechanical device. It would, indeed, seem highly dangerous, if not impossible, to copy directly the model of a social institution—and in America counselling is one—from another country. If it is flourishing in the other country, as counselling is in the U.S., one has to ask oneself what functional rôle the institution fulfils there, in what kind of educational and social situation it was found to supply a need so that it gained support for its growth and establishment. The need to analyse this situation is my excuse for reverting briefly again to the United States.

How counselling arose in the United States

The definition of 'guidance and counselling' given by Maurice Craft (see page 9) will serve very well as an anchor for our discussion.

The secondary school counsellor is, in fact, one of the recurring identities marking the American educational scene across the states. By now there will be the equivalent of about 30,000 full-time counsellors in the schools (though not all are, in fact, full-time counsellors). How did this service come to boom into such an industry? Counsellors have been introduced into the schools mainly since the last war. Tyler's 'combination of a diversified society with democratic ideals' (see page 14)—for her the basic *raison d'être* for American counsellors—can in the high schools be translated by 'the diversified curriculum' which provides a very solid reason for their existence. It is considered an inseparable part of the democratic nature of the school to allow each pupil to choose from a very wide variety of different courses (over two hundred in many schools I know), and so make up his own time-table, and this choice is remade every year or even half-year. A subject may be taken for a year or two, then dropped and possibly taken up again later, and innumerable combinations of different subjects and varying levels are, in theory, possible. This is what Conant (1967) means by 'the elective program'. It would, indeed, be very difficult for a pupil simply to find his way, unaided, through this maze of curricular offerings and even more so to make a choice that is meaningful in terms of his own aims and needs. As this system developed, it clearly thus became necessary for a selected teacher to assume responsibility for guiding the student through the multiplicity of choices. Whilst the American school counsellor can trace his ancestry also to the vocational guidance worker of previous decades, he owes his widespread existence primarily then to the stucture and curricular system of the American school.

The impetus for the really large-scale expansion of the new profession came with the alarm and concern about the state of education following in the wake of the first Sputnik. Official America became very concerned to search out the existing talent of the nation. Guidance and counselling services were seen as a useful means towards this end and hence encouraged both in the spirit and financially by national legislation, especially the *National Defense Education Act, 1958.*

The other aspect of counselling, 'mental-health or personality-centred' counselling, was superimposed on the first function, partly as a result of increasing interest in psychological adjustment, partly under the influence of university training departments. While this function in fact still takes second place in schools, it has been gaining ground over recent years.

Counselling in America, as I see it, is part of the pattern of manifold educational choices. It is a service made necessary in the first place by the complexity of the school system which has engendered considerable specialisation of functions amongst teachers in the school, and counselling is one manifestation of this specialisation. It is also a means of discovering, developing and guiding the talents of the nation and thus serves the economic aims of the state. But it is more than this: it is, in addition, a form of personal service or help for the psychologically lame and the underprivileged; it forms an integral part of the numerous special projects that have been set up to ensure that opportunities become more equal as parts of the 'War on Poverty'. It is, in a way, a sign that an open society adheres to an optimistic belief in the perfectibility of the human race.

Needs in Britain

How do we in Britain stand in relation to this? How far do our needs and our educational situation coincide with those of the United States so that similar remedies may be called for?

The most obvious *difference* lies in the school structure; in Britain educational choices are far fewer and are remade less frequently than in the United States, even though our secondary schools are growing steadily more complex. Hence, the kind of specialist guide for educational courses is needed to a far lesser extent and certainly not on anything like the scale thought suitable in America (one counsellor to two hundred and fifty students). If this was the only function the trained counsellor could fulfil we would not need him. Also, the degree of specialisation of functions—if you like, 'bureaucratisation'—has proceeded less far in British schools and our manpower resources are more meagre. Hence we must inevitably regard more cautiously the employment of full-time specialists.

On the other hand, there are some clear needs in our schools which, I suggest, are not at the moment being fully met. Chapter One of this book sets out clearly a technological society's increasing need for guidance on educational and vocational choices, if true equality of opportunity is to be achieved. The guidance in this area given in our schools at the present moment is generally deficient in scope and lacks a systematic, professional approach. Moreover, the help given by teachers to adolescents in the wider area of their relations to themselves, their families and society—in the sphere of emotional and social adjustment— needs, I suggest, to be deepened and made more all-embracing— and not only for the ulterior purpose of avoiding wastage of ability. Links with the home, naturally, form an integral part of this.

An awareness that help in this field needs to be more thorough is, in fact, already growing in educational circles and various expedients are being adopted up and down the country. A. W. Rowe and Helen Whale have described two of the more successful schemes. In other areas 'school social workers' have been appointed—or sometimes they are called people in charge of 'pastoral care'. Under other schemes, outsiders come into the schools to hold discussion groups on 'personal relations' (the modern euphemism for 'sex education'), and discussions are extended on an individual basis to other personal problems, as in the 'Avondale Project' in London. The variety of arrangements adopted is a tribute to the fertility of human inventiveness; the result, without proper evaluation of their effectiveness, I venture to suggest is chaos.

Skills

The common feature of most of these schemes (though not of all of them) is that the people involved lack any special training or skills. Now, people have confided in one another for thousands of years and this has an important part to play in the relieving of human predicaments. We must not underestimate the enormous potentialities for good in an understanding relationship between an individual pupil and an adult with whom he 'clicks'. As one American teenage girl put it to me—in a school that had a generous complement of very competent counsellors:

> I wouldn't go to 'my' counsellor; I would rather go to my last year's French teacher. I'm much more intellectually close to him.

The amateur approach has, of course, always had its warm advocates in England—in government service, as well as in education. However, there are certain difficulties and it is a sign of the times that the Fulton Committee on the Civil Service, for instance, has acknowledged that the gifted layman in the higher echelons of administration is 'an obsolete cult'. When it is said that the tutor of a 'tutor group' or the housemaster combines all the counselling that is necessary with all his other duties, I suspect that lip service is being paid to its desirability rather than that this help exists in reality. Certainly my own experience as a class teacher would bear out the contention that the class teacher's position as well as lack of time would normally work against any really deep-going counselling.

The right personality is indeed the *prime* requisite in this field of work. A well-known American counsellor educator has written:

> Training for a counsellor is the icing on a cake which is already quite appetising! (Arbuckle, 1967a)

All training departments in universities take account of this fact and attach corresponding importance to personality factors in selection though this kind of judgement is notoriously fallible. However, it is becoming recognised also that special skills are involved and that the best personality will function better *with* rather than without training.

There is, I think, a certain resistance to the introduction of professionalised, skilled help in the schools which is based on the fear that this will lead to a restriction, a diminution in the teacher's rôle—the fear that something is being taken away from him. However, this need not be so; such help can, in fact, assist every teacher in the school to carry out his educative rôle more effectively and more skilfully. Certainly, a somewhat new rôle has to be fitted into the existing structure of the school and relations have to be worked out between the counsellor, the head-teacher and other members of staff, as well as between coun-sellor and outside agencies. But I feel there are no difficulties that could not be surmounted given some tact and goodwill.

A professional approach in the best sense means that the worker is aware of his own limitations and knows when to call in further help. It means that problems are handled at least com-petently, and that well-intentioned but potentially dangerous blunders may more often be avoided. The possession of pro-fessional skills also bestows on the worker some confidence in his own worth and knowledge, and thus renders him less dependent on quick emotional rewards which are seldom forth-coming.

I write with somewhat less assurance about the need for professional skills in 1968 than I would have done one or two years earlier, because of some recent research that has demon-strated the effectiveness of non-professional workers in the field of psychotherapy. For instance, a study by Poser, reported in Cartwright (1968), found that when male schizophrenic patients in a hospital were randomly assigned to therapy groups conducted by young untrained college girls and by trained psychiatrists and P.S.W's, the patients 'treated' by the untrained girls showed greater improvement. It may indeed well be that minimally trained people can be effective if closely supported by more thoroughly trained professionals. Nevertheless, the need for training is felt perhaps most acutely by people who have been put into such situations without preparation.

The skills that we try to develop as part of this professional training are many, but these are some of the more important ones:

1. An attitude that avoids judging the client, that accepts him with his imperfections—a non-moralising attitude.
2. Understanding the client even beyond his superficial words—'perceiving the client's psychological world' as Leona Tyler puts it.
3. Communicating this acceptance and understanding to the client.
4. Helping the client to find out about and explore his aims, needs, capabilities—by means of tests as well as talk.

To enumerate these skills is easy enough, to practise them a great deal more difficult, for all of us, even after years of experience. We attempt to help counselling students to approximate to them above all by means of counselling practice in schools which is tape-recorded and later discussed at the University. In addition, of course, they acquire a great deal of theoretical background in sociology, psychology and testing which will inform their work and make it more purposeful and coherent.

The future

What of the future?

The present model of the counsellor as we train him in the various university courses—and they are very similar in purpose and content—is largely based on the present American university concept of the counsellor who is expected to combine the three strands of counselling. However, this need not be the final model; it is a useful stage at a time when we are introducing a new concept and are not sure how and in what form it will 'take' in our culture, and perhaps it is as necessary as the chrysalis stage is necessary for the development of the mature butterfly.

If one examines the situation in America and then looks at the different types of social agencies available in this country doubts begin to arise—doubts that are concerned with the alignment of functions between the different helping professions. Doubts centre firstly on the combination of educational-vocational and personal-social counselling functions in the same person, and secondly on the piecemeal growth of separate disciplines, all dealing in some degree with personal-social counselling.

The 'Holy Trinity' of counselling—educational, vocational and personal—exists more in theory than in practice in the United States. In reality, American school counsellors hardly ever combine the three functions. They are most heavily involved in educational guidance, i.e. helping the pupil find the right combination of courses at school or choose the appropriate university.

In fact, the interaction between counsellor and pupil on educational choices will usually be of a routine character and will be kept at a mundane level. Very rarely will such an encounter provide an opportunity for branching out into more deeply personal explorations. Personal-social counselling even on more normal adolescent problems is therefore on the whole fairly minimal. (For the sake of brevity I have to oversimplify, but by and large this is true, although there are exceptions.) The reasons for the absence of personal counselling are probably many. There is the lack of time in view of frequently heavy involvement in administrative tasks and educational 'slotting'; there may be cursory training in the past which has left the counsellor with insufficient confidence in his own competence in this area. Some counsellors may indeed 'escape' into routine clerical work because of a realisation of their limitations. But there is doubtless also the inherent difficulty of combining the functions of educational counselling where administrative decisions have eventually to be arrived at—and are often taken by the counsellor himself—and of the more personal counselling in the social and emotional sphere. The duality of the counsellor's rôle is in fact seen as an inhibiting factor by many American students, who perceive the two rôles as contradictory, one detracting from the other (cf. Lytton, 1968).

If we look, then, for a more natural fold into which these different functions can fall, it seems most appropriate perhaps to separate off the decision-making, or decision-facilitating, relatively *cognitive* function from the relatively *emotional* one, i.e. to split off the vocational-educational counselling from the personal-social counselling. This is a division that would, I think, come most naturally to the majority of non-counsellors, at any rate, and that would, in fact, also follow an existing allotment of functions in the *British* as opposed to the American educational system. Each of these functions, it might be thought, would appeal to a different kind of personality so that because of the more circumscribed nature of the job the task of selecting the right personnel would become clearer. May I then suggest that educational and vocational guidance is best carried out by teachers, who would act part-time or in a full-time capacity and who would be given much more systematic training than hitherto in assessment procedures. Such vocational advisers would be familiar with the psychology of occupational development and the determinants of occupational choice, and they would be bound to view the student's vocational aims in the light of his overall aptitudes, needs and interests; in other words, in the light of his total personality.

It is perhaps necessary, in these days of publicity for mental health, to emphasise the importance of vocational counselling. In general importance, it is at least the equal of psychotherapy since it represents a kind of assistance that can be of enormous help in the development of *every individual*. Patterson (1964) writes:

> ... there seems to be some utility in continuing the term 'vocational counselling'. First, it is well to recognise the desirability of focusing upon a particular area—or problem—in an individual's life. This does not mean that other areas are ignored, or that the counsellor does not deal with a whole human being. Second, an adequate concept of vocational counselling should not rule out consideration of attitudinal and emotional factors in vocational development and choice. Third, such a concept recognises that many individuals have problems in the area of vocational choice that are not symptoms of general maladjustment or emotional disturbance. Fourth, the concept is useful in that it indicates distinctions between the handling of vocational problems and the handling of other kinds of problems ...

> The rise of interest in psychotherapy, emphasising as it does these factors (of emotions and attitudes), has sometimes seemed to threaten to drive vocational counselling out of existence. Certainly, as conceived and practised earlier (i.e. giving attention to cognitive factors only) vocational counselling can no longer expect to survive.

> But the alternative is not the absorption of vocational counselling by psychotherapy. The need is for a revitalising of vocational counselling by changing the model from a cognitive one, not to a psychotherapy model, but to a composite, more realistic model which recognises the importance of emotions, feelings and attitudes in the normal vocational development process.

This is precisely the work that I am proposing for the future vocational adviser. To carry it out effectively he will need some training in minimal counselling so that he will take account of all the factors that motivate his client's choices, and so that he does not fall into the trap of simply providing him with information. But it must be recognised that there exist many problems of personality and poor adjustment to the environment which are outside his scope and which he need not be trained to deal with. The blocking of the ego-function of the under-achiever, personality difficulties resulting in problems of adjustment to school, seeking a sense of identity, all these are examples of such problems that fall outside his realm and that illustrate typical problems of personal-social adjustment, some of which may be more and some less 'normal'.

Let us now look at the area of personal counselling.

Indeed, the process of working with these problems is entangled in a profusion and confusion of terms. In my experience the same process of helping an individual with his personal adjustment that is called 'therapy' when carried out by a psychiatrist or clinical psychologist, is called 'casework' when it is done by a social worker and 'counselling' when done by a counsellor. What does casework in fact involve? This is a description provided by a social worker:

> . . . when casework is employed to help the individual achieve better social functioning it becomes a form of psycho-social therapy. It relies mainly on rational procedures closely allied to psychoanalytic techniques, augmented by methods of direct influence when diagnosis indicates that these will be more effective. Focus is always upon the person-situation gestalt, which is seen as an interacting balance of forces between the needs of the person and the influence upon him of the environment. (Hollis, 1964.)

Leaving aside the 'psychoanalytic techniques', is this any different from what the counsellor purports to do?

Let us look at the functions that each of the professions of psychologist, social worker, and counsellor claims for itself. In the following quotations from the American literature a few identifying phrases have been omitted.

> No. 1. Assist each pupil to meet the needs and understand himself in relation to the social and psychological world in which he lives . . . Assist all members of the staff to understand the importance of the individual pupil . . . Determine the influence of the school program on pupil educational and psychological development . . . Inform other staff members of significant changes in the school and non-school environments which have implications . . . Assist parents to understand the developmental progress of their child, his needs and environmental opportunities . . .

> No. 2. . . . understanding, and providing help, within the program of the school, for children who are having difficulties in using the resources of the school effectively . . . an approach . . . based on his understanding of human behavior, his skill in relationship and interviewing, and his ability to use school and community resources.

> No. 3. . . . psychological counseling and guidance with such specific activities as individual child guidance, individual parent counseling, student counseling groups and parent discussion groups; consultation, with such activities as consulting with individual teachers, teacher discussion groups, research and educational development, and referral and community services; individual and psychological evaluation, including such activities as case study, examination, diagnoses, recommending, reporting and follow-up procedures. (Arbuckle, 1967b.)

One might be forgiven for thinking that all three quotations relate to one profession. In fact, the first one refers to secondary school counsellors, the second to social workers and the third to psychologists. The overlap in claims (though not in actual functions in secondary schools) is alarming and one wonders what justification there is in keeping these workers separate in training and function.

Inevitably, wherever difficulties exist for the individual, personal problems, behaviour and learning problems are closely interrelated and any effective help will have to touch on them all. In this area the 'normal' imperceptibly merges into the 'abnormal', it is notoriously difficult to draw a borderline and there is a considerable field in which skills overlap. One might of course maintain that we in this country can avoid the American confusion and multiplicity of workers in schools quite easily by simply not creating the new professions of 'counsellor' or 'school social worker'. Schools have at their disposal services, centrally based and organised by the local authority, that are intended to help precisely with difficulties of this kind. There are the child guidance and the school psychological services, the child care and the probation services.

But is the provision of such highly qualified personnel adequate to meet the need, or is it likely to be adequate in the future? At present these services deal with the more acute and more serious cases. They could not hope to deal with *normal* problems of adolescent adjustment and the child guidance and school psychological services, for instance, function much more extensively in primary than in secondary schools. The school staff, after all, have a particularly good vantage point to detect the signs of incipient disturbance in a pupil whom they see daily, and to intervene in its development hopefully at an early stage.

Not to introduce some more skilled help would mean denying the call for greater and more systematic help in meeting adolescents' social and emotional needs. It would mean turning our backs on the widespread movement to pay greater attention to the area of 'personal growth' or 'education for personal relations' or 'social education' which is important, particularly in the *educational priority areas*. These problems are ours as much as they are those of the United States. I am suggesting that this movement cannot be halted and the call will have to be met in some way. But we are able to learn from American 'mistakes'; we are in the fortunate position of being able to act with hindsight. In this way, and with the advantage of well-developed child guidance and child care services, we might well leap across fifteen years of their development and start where they are now rather than introduce in 1970 a counsellor model that was appropriate in the early 'fifties.

Schools up and down the country are calling for 'school social workers' or 'counsellors' to help them solve some of their problems in the area of social education. What we have to realise is that these new helpers by whatever name they go, as well as the educational psychologists who already exist, although in minute numbers, are all pursuing identical aims with very similar techniques *where they wish to promote the personal growth or adjustment of the individual.* The recognition of this fact is only now dawning in the United States with all that it implies for the preparation and training of these workers. What conclusion is being drawn from this? In a recent paper, Arbuckle (1967b) writes:

> Thus I would propose an ecumenical movement between those departments, schools, or colleges in universities that are involved in the education of the school counselor, the school social worker and the school psychologist. If a certain level of competency in the area of appraisal of personality traits, or certain capacities in therapeutic counseling, or certain knowledges about man, his behavior, and the culture in which he lives, are considered to be minimal requirements, we might wonder why we should have three different departments, all providing the same basic educational experience to satisfy these requirements. If one department provides a much superior experience in any one area, why not do away with the other two and use the superior way for all three?

Indeed, an Interprofessional Research Commission has been set up in the United States to investigate and improve collaboration between the different services and to increase their effectiveness. Under its aegis the University of Michigan is experimenting with common core training for counsellors, nurses, social workers and school psychologists. It is hoped that if they are trained at least in part together, people will learn to co-operate and respect the skills of other professional groups. In the more distant future this may indeed lead to a merging of disciplines. Is it too fanciful to hope that we, too, might draw the logical conclusion from the situation, that the future with us, too, might see experiments in training that has a common core content for the present three disciplines? Then the extent to which each of the three would be involved in individual or group counselling with the child would depend as much on the person and his educational background as it would on his occupational title. In other words, the main factor here would be the depth and quality of the person's professional education. I am not suggesting this will come today or tomorrow, but it may well be a vision of the more distant future.

The logic of this development would then lead eventually to the emergence of one generalist worker, call him 'Pupil Welfare Worker' or 'Pupil Personnel Worker', or preferably something more elegant. He would be based inside the school and would combine, at a general practitioner level, most of the functions and skills of the present-day counsellor, school social worker and educational psychologist. To acquire these skills he would no doubt need two years' specialised training. A 'Pupil Personnel Worker' trained for psychological counselling would add greatly to the school's effectiveness in promoting its pupils' personal development. At the same time he would have to be backed by a strong 'Social Service Department'. A unified 'Social Service Department' such as the Seebohm Committee (Seebohm, 1968) is recommending, would be a centrally based local authority service containing all the existing disciplines with perhaps somewhat modified functions. This service would provide more highly trained personnel: child psychiatrist, educational or child psychologist, psychiatric social worker, child care worker, etc. It would act as a referral and consultant resource to schools and their pupil personnel workers, as well as to the community in general. The Pupil Personnel Workers in the schools would refer certain children to the specialist services and would discuss others with it on a consultant basis. The activities of the school-based personnel would naturally have to be co-ordinated with those of the 'Social Service Department' to avoid the familiar bogy of seventeen different workers all descending on one deserving family.

This kind of solution is still in the distant future in the United States. It will perhaps be said it is completely Utopian here, given our financial and organisational circumstances. Nor, of course, is it the only possible solution. What we certainly need are experiments with different kinds of organisation, well controlled and set up, so that we can evaluate in an objective fashion the effects of each type.

This is a vision of the future. Meanwhile, there is the present and meanwhile the counsellors we are training now—the present model—have an important function to fulfil. Nor must we forget that the teacher who is untrained, but has the right personality and approach, has enormous value by the side of the trained specialist—even where these are plentiful, as in the United States. In various ways we are groping towards our aim. The more diversified and complex our society, the more complex the schools, the greater the need for help if the school is to carry out its task of guiding the young in their personal, as well as their intellectual development.

A Comment on Chapter Seven

R. Leslie Reid

May I begin by saying that I have no special knowledge of any form of counselling, and that my comments are primarily those of an outsider, a member of the general ('non-counselling') public, and secondarily those of an academic psychologist, 'pure' in the nowadays derogatory sense of the word. Fortunately for me, in his paper Dr. Lytton chose to discuss some of the more general and fundamental problems rather than matters of detail and technique. I am sure that his concern with the broad strategy of development is wise and proper at the present stage. It is all too easy simply to see a job that needs doing, and to rush in and improvise ways of doing it that fit local circumstances. While this may lead to a variety of approaches and so provide the necessary conditions for an evolutionary type of development, a considered policy for the future is also needed to restrain the creation of vested interests that may later act as barriers to co-operation. One of the most important functions of this symposium could be to help to move towards a general consensus of opinion about the main lines of policy. We have to think for ourselves rather than follow in the wake of the United States because we operate within a different society, one that is more rigid in its organisation and employment, in which educational and vocational choices are fewer but earlier and more binding, and in which we place more faith in the amateur with an inborn flair and less in the expert with special training.

Dr. Lytton has given particular attention to the three different functions of the counsellor: educational, vocational, and personal. With this, as with the other Holy Trinity, I have the greatest difficulty over the last item. I am troubled by the suggestion that personal counselling should be carried out by a specialist, leaving the rest to teachers. This seems like giving away the bread-and-butter and keeping the jam. As an outsider I would like to see counsellors, as a new professional group, offering an obvious, straightforward practical service to the community. The element of conspicuous utility is not present in the pure counselling function. I am not simply thinking of those who control the strings of the public purse but also of the counsellors themselves. The job must be varied and satisfying if it is to appeal to the man who wants a career rather than the pioneering enthusiast. Would it be wise to give away the part that offers the best opportunity for immediate rewards and the display of special skill and knowledge?

Part of the discussion following the paper was concerned with the reasons for advocating a split such as Dr. Lytton had suggested, particularly the possible conflict between the advisory and the non-directive therapeutic rôles. The point was made that in practice, personal counselling was always directive to some degree although usually less so than in vocational guidance, and some members of the audience were wary of 'semantic problems' raised by the term 'directive'. It is not obvious to an outsider that there should be any real conflict between the different functions of a counsellor. Vocational *selection* would create conflict because the candidate and the interviewer are in opposition, but in the guidance situation the counsellor offers aid to the candidate in making his own choice of career and their interests are identical.

As an academic psychologist I am concerned about the relationship between pure and applied psychology. The counsellor must be a craftsman prepared to work by intuition and rule of thumb, but at the same time he should be regarded as an applied psychologist and I would hope that in the future he may come to be supported by a more adequate corpus of scientific knowledge. As far as personal counselling is concerned, one obstacle to progress is that the aims lack precise definition. To aim at 'promoting the personal growth or adjustment of the individual' without going on to indicate how such a thing can be measured, or at least reliably assessed, is to stop short of the point at which scientific knowledge can be put to use. Even the improvement of techniques at pre-scientific level depends upon having a definite purpose and knowing how far it is being achieved. It is possible to find some theoretical justification for almost any approach to personal counselling. For example, one might argue that young people in our present society have enough

94

opportunities for talking things over in a permissive atmosphere, that what they most lack are clear ideals and strong moral imperatives, and that in consequence a counsellor should set out to give strong and definite advice together with assistance in carrying it out. Arguments of this kind for any particular approach, and the enthusiasm and sense of achievement of its practitioners cannot be accepted in lieu of objective evidence that the approach is effective in achieving some defined aim. Until the problem of assessment of results is given the highest priority, fashion in personal counselling can simply replace fashion with no evident progress.

Now I should perhaps deal with one point that Dr. Lytton has been too tactful to mention. As an academic psychologist I am keenly aware of the deficiencies of my own discipline as a support for the various kinds of applied psychology. The annual crop of degree examinations makes me wish that the questions could be put in a different form. Within the subject there are by now a few areas in which it is just possible to set problems for solution so that the candidate can demonstrate what he can do with what he knows, but most of the questions can only take the form of inviting discussion of some problem rather than requiring its solution. Apart from this, much of psychology is remote and perhaps rather dull because it is intended to provide answers to questions that psychologists themselves have raised rather than questions that practical people consider to be important. For their part, the practitioners have not been sufficiently ready to ask for assistance from the pure psychologist and so to impose proper demands on psychological research. The gap is unfortunate for the parties on both sides of it, and more contact between counsellors and university departments would help to reduce it.

Future conferences will no doubt return to many of the issues that Dr. Lytton has raised. While he has proposed a solution to the organisational problem by the creation of 'Pupil Personnel Workers', a proposal that has the conspicuous merit of preventing different specialists from treading on each others' toes, I believe that as an academic psychologist and a practitioner he is more concerned with his final recommendation for experimental trials of different kinds of organisation, set up so that an objective evaluation can be made of the effects of each type. On this subject there can be no room for argument except about the means by which the objective can be achieved.

8. Some Practical Issues

C. James Gill

This chapter outlines and comments on some of the questions raised and views expressed at the two final sessions of the conference, during which a group of practising school counsellors and most of the conference speakers answered questions.

Although guidance and counselling in this country frequently provides a topic of discussion at conferences of teachers, the employment of trained school counsellors is in its infancy, and the future rôle of counsellors in secondary schools has begun to be worked out in practice only in the last two or three years. When, therefore, men and women from different parts of the educational system are invited to talk on 'The School Counsellor' from their differing viewpoints a consensus can scarcely be expected, and the list of duties they consider a counsellor might reasonably undertake is likely to extend beyond the capacity and powers of any one person. This, while raising questions of priorities for the counsellor, should be reassuring to those teachers fearful of losing their responsibility for pastoral care to a new kind of professional service within the school; there is obviously plenty for all to do if the needs of individual pupils are to be met more fully; and even in schools where there is a strong tradition of pastoral care it is generally conceded that more could be done to help boys and girls to deal with the problems they meet in the normal course of development at school, among their friends and in the home.

It must be emphasised that counsellors are not concerned solely with problem children, in fact their main concern is for children with problems or who are in some temporary emotional difficulty or personal predicament. The problems are usually described as educational, vocational, social or personal, and some members of the conference doubted whether a counsellor could be competent in all these areas. What is certain is the inability of a counsellor to take over the continuous day-to-day responsibility for the welfare of children exercised by subject teachers, housemasters/mistresses, tutors and others. A counsellor cannot do his work effectively without the help and support of the head and staff; with their co-operation he can add to the available resources of knowledge, insight, time and skill for helping troubled boys and girls; his presence in a school could increase the awareness of the staff to the difficulties and anxieties of pupils and lead to a deepening of pastoral care.

Members of the conference asked how a counsellor was introduced into a school, how staff, children and parents heard about him and learned of his place and purpose in the school. It is usual for heads to inform the staff either in a staff meeting or by describing on paper before the arrival of the counsellor some of the main responsibilities he will assume at the start, with some indication of possible future developments. A counsellor is sometimes introduced at a staff meeting where he can briefly indicate his own view of his place in the school and invite suggestions from the staff on ways in which he might add to his usefulness. Individual discussions with members of staff are also found to be productive of understanding and good relations. One way of getting to know the pupils is to see all those of a certain year group, for example, all those entering the school for their first year, or those making an educational choice at the end of the second or third year, or those faced with career decisions in the fourth year. In general it has been found advisable for a counsellor to become established in a school slowly, taking account of the organisation and the form of delegation of responsibility for welfare and pastoral care in individual schools.

Among teething troubles are excessive referrals of troublesome pupils by the staff, and the trying out of the counsellor by pupils curious to learn about the reactions of the new member of staff. On the whole the counsellors had found themselves accepted fairly quickly, especially by the pupils, and they were agreed there was a tendency for the percentage of self-referrals to grow once the counsellor was established in the school. Several methods of referral had been tried, from an informal direct approach to the counsellor by the pupil to interviews arranged in response to a signed request from an individual, the time of the appointment being agreed with the appropriate member of staff.

There has to be some flexibility to allow for emergencies. The counsellor has to be accessible to children in unexpected difficulties or under unusual strain, and responsive to requests for help from members of staff.

There are differing views on whether a counsellor should teach or not. For example, one said she had no difficulty in being permissive in a counselling interview and a disciplinarian in the classroom; another found that teaching kept her in touch with both staff and pupils; another suggested that even if pupils found the dual rôle acceptable, most counsellors would have difficulty in adjusting to it. As good teachers, counsellors naturally regret the loss of the continuous contact with groups of children that class teaching gives, and they might make their contribution to the curriculum and economise in the use of their time by taking sessions for group guidance dealing with, say, personal relations, preparation for entering the adult world on leaving school, and careers information. A wide range of problems could be discussed together and from these discussions requests for individual counselling would no doubt arise. Quite apart from the question of rôle conflict, experience already gained shows that the time required to deal with the needs uncovered by counsellors is such as to justify the whole of one person's work being committed to counselling in a secondary school, certainly in a school of 800 or more pupils. There is also much to be said in favour of having someone in the school outside the usual departmental and authority structure, to whom boys and girls can turn for help and with whom they can establish a relationship from which they can withdraw when support is no longer needed.

Some members of the conference warned of the danger of self-exploration leading to serious introspection: by discovering new problems boys and girls might develop new anxieties. It seems likely that a few days spent in counselling would suffice to confirm the existence of enough real problems without imaginary ones being created, but counsellors in their concern for helping with personal problems, some of which stem from home conditions, should certainly be on their guard against invading the privacy of the individual or the privacy of the home. Some counsellors readily visit parents in their homes while others prefer to see them at school and make time available for interviews during the day or in the evening. Counsellors would normally be well advised not to visit a home unless the boy or girl concerned had agreed, otherwise the intervention of the counsellor with the parent might be interpreted as an attempt to put pressure on the pupil. Besides, the conflicts causing difficulties for children in many homes cannot so easily be resolved; a counsellor should not lightly enter a family situation to attempt to do what would tax the skill and understanding of a trained family case-worker.

Having a counsellor on a school staff makes possible a closer liaison with outside guidance agencies—the child guidance clinic, the youth employment service, child care workers, the school psychologist and others. From frequent contact with outside specialists the counsellor gains in experience of when to refer and when not to refer pupils for specialist help, and can also enlist the co-operation of members of staff to give support to individual pupils in a way most likely to assist the efforts of specialists working outside the school setting. The danger of over-taxing present referral services is apparent. There seems to be little point in further lengthening the queues awaiting access to the services of the school psychologist or the psychiatrist. Perhaps the way ahead is to train counsellors as general practitioners to work within the school and also gradually to strengthen the outside agencies which can give specialist services. Later, counsellors themselves might be trained more deeply in psychology, if indeed the development lies in the direction of a division of function between educational, vocational, and personal counsellors.

Counsellors themselves appear to be agreed that personal counselling has so far proved to be the most successful part of their work and is for them the most satisfying. For them, too, the most valuable part of their training as counsellors consisted of those experiences that deepen their self-understanding; practical counselling is of great importance in training, and the analysis of interviews which have been taped is valuable in many ways, not least in helping the counsellor himself to increase his self-understanding.

Confidentiality is not found to be a serious difficulty in practice, though many teachers find difficulty in accepting the theoretical position. Pupils must have no doubts on the maintenance of confidentiality, otherwise the counselling relationship cannot be established on a basis of trust. Information given to a counsellor in a confidential interview should be within the control of the pupil and should not be divulged to other members of staff without his consent. When boys and girls seek help, through self-referral, it is unusual for them to object to bringing others who might help into consultation—the head, other members of staff or parents—to find some solution to their problems or to help them in making decisions. Frequently, having 'laid their problem on the table' and looked at it objectively, they are themselves willing to discuss it with other people who might help, whereas previously, such was their emotional involvement, they were inclined to avoid bringing it into the open. As an adult member of the school community the counsellor has responsibilities to the head and staff, and where the well-being of the pupil or the school is endangered, as in the use of drugs, action might have to be taken without a pupil's agreement.* If pupils in need are to be given support by members of staff, some feed-back of information to the staff is essential and this can usually be achieved without any breach of confidentiality. Close co-operation with heads is important and can achieve a two-way supply of information advantageous to individuals and to the school community as a whole.

As the schools become more concerned to help boys and girls to look ahead and prepare themselves to handle those rôles and relationships involved in the next stage of development, whether in school or outside the school, at home, among their friends or at work, the keeping of cumulative records to build up an all-round picture of the individual and his development becomes more important. There is no point in keeping records unless some decision has been taken on their usefulness. Counsellors in the course of their work may need to record information of a personal nature and this should be made as a private note or aide-mémoire; as such it is a confidential paper for the counsellor's private use. Factual information only should be entered on the school's cumulative record card since this is a record made as a normal part of the work of a school and it might on occasion be required in evidence.

Developmental counselling, by which a pupil is helped to plan ahead and prepare himself to handle those rôles and relationships he will meet in the next stage of development, e.g. in work, at university or technical college, was mentioned in

* *The Criminal Law Act, 1967,* has, however, brought about a change in the law so that it is no longer an offence if someone does not disclose to the police an offence known to him, so long as he does not accept ⅃ reward for his silence. (The Eds.)

discussion, and so was the concept of vocational development as an aspect of personal development. To make decisions individuals need to have a degree of self-understanding and some knowledge of the area of choice; this suggests a deliberate attempt on the part of the school to provide opportunities for individuals to explore work possibilities and a range of subjects before they have to make decisions on higher or further education or employment. 'Exploration without commitment' is really another version of 'planned procrastination'.

Since counsellors seek to deepen self-knowledge and to help young people in their personal relations there might be a case for introducing a course of elementary psychology into the school curriculum. Such a course might be useful if it had an experimental basis and included a study of perception and ways of learning, but it could be argued that some subjects are better started at university and psychology is one of them. Sociology, too, might contribute towards, say, an examination of prejudices through a study of the cultural setting and the social system.

The client-centred, non-directive approach to counselling associated with Carl Rogers underlay much of the discussion during the conference, for example, when non-directive counselling was contrasted with directive or authoritarian teaching; but there are good arguments for other theories of counselling such as directive, existentialist, developmental or behavioural. At one point in the discussion two interviews to illustrate the difference between non-directive and behavioural counselling were quoted from an article by Robert H. Woody (1968). Each interview starts with a boy saying: 'What I wanted to talk to you about was getting a job. I'll be leaving school in a few months and I really don't know what I would like to do.' The non-directive counsellor allows the boy to establish the direction of the interview and to leave the topic of vocational choice to talk about his mother's illness and its consequences. In contrast, the behavioural counsellor refuses to reinforce talk about the mother's illness and gives positive reinforcement when the boy makes a response related to vocational choice.

But how did the behavioural counsellor know that a vocational choice was the boy's main counselling objective? He might have been so deeply disturbed by his mother's illness that he was in no condition to make a vocational decision until he had come to terms with it and its consequences, such as the necessity of taking more responsibility in the home. The example actually illustrated the contribution a counsellor can make by helping boys or girls to clarify their problems, and when they know what is relevant to their needs they are in a better position to profit from the help and information available from other members of staff, or outside agencies such as subject teachers, tutors, careers staff or youth employment officers. The article quoted concludes that there should not be such a person as a behavioural counsellor; 'rather there should be counsellors who are well-trained generically and who can use behavioural techniques appropriately as part of their array of professional skills'. Whatever approaches a counsellor uses he must remain true to himself. Differences of view there will be; this must not be mistaken for confusion.

9. Postscript

Hugh Lytton

In the preceding chapters of this symposium references to American literature and practice in counselling abound and one becomes impressed with how much we in Britain are indebted to that country for the concepts, the careful elaboration of techniques and the very terminology which we employ in this new profession. The primary significance of the conference from which this book arose, as I see it, lies in the fact that it marked an advance in the process of weaning ourselves from the overwhelming transatlantic influence, while acknowledging our debt to it. Through the conference, I think counselling in Britain has taken a step, however small, on the road of fashioning its own identity and evolving in a way that is sensitive to British needs and to our situation, educational, economic and social. For we have an educational philosophy of our own in which the pupil's welfare plays no small part; nor do we lack techniques though they may not be as sharply or as thoroughly worked out as in the United States and may go under other names. I am thinking particularly in this connection of the procedures used for many years by our Child Guidance Clinics and other social work agencies.

It is always difficult to pinpoint exactly the first signs and causes of a nascent movement. The social, educational and psychological climate—as expressed in the growing complexity and specialisation of society, the rise of the comprehensive schools and an increasing concern with personal and social adjustment—have all contributed to the emergence of counselling in Britain. But on a more concrete level there have been forces of an individual and organisational kind, each travelling along its own path and interacting but distantly, that have, almost in a fit of absent-mindedness, put counselling on the educational map. Academics in colleges and universities, some psychologists and social workers recognised that the increasing diversity of our society and of our educational arrangements required more thorough provision of personal help for pupils. Many head-teachers came to realise that the social, educational and personal problems in comprehensive schools would not solve themselves and would be beyond them to cope with, and the more far-sighted amongst them began to ask for help in the social work field. The National Association for Mental Health and the Gulbenkian Trust acted as catalysts by gathering together interested people and jointly sponsoring invitation conferences in 1963 and 1966. The Gulbenkian Trust also materially assisted the development of the first counselling course at Keele University and the N.A.M.H. instituted a Working Party on the subject. These organisations, as well as the International Round Tables for Vocational and Educational Guidance and Counselling organised by Mr. H. Hoxter, Youth Employment Officer for the Borough of Newham, all facilitated the development and crystallisation of these ideas, new to Britain in this form. Many teachers—and psychologists and youth employment officers—however, have remained sceptical.

The questions that surround the problematical and controversial subject of counselling have many times been discussed in smaller, local meetings, as well as at the private conferences mentioned above. But at this conference at Exeter they were probably for the first time discussed at national level in public. Private worrying about these problems gave way to a public statement and exploration of the issues involved. It seems to me that the first function the conference performed for most participants was to clarify some facts and issues, specify the problems, bring them into greater focus, and even to define more precisely the terminology in common use: a function of clarification.

The second function was to provide a meeting place for a wide range of professionals from all over the country where they could exchange experiences and take stock of what was already being done in this sphere. They could discuss their common interest in counselling and their difficulties, as well as express their nagging doubts and uncertainties. This was done at question time in the plenary sessions, as well as in small discussion groups and in the open forum at the end of the conference.

What are the prominent themes that come to the fore in the contributions to this book?

Counselling has in some ways been like the proverbial elephant of which we have all been blindly describing different parts without granting the validity of each other's descriptions. A tentative definition of what counselling is—and is not—about is therefore a primary need and forms one of the first themes of the symposium. However, as the chapters unfold, this skeleton, in being covered with flesh, is given life and invested with reality and it is seen that the definition—transatlantic in origin— has received subtle twists in an English direction and that it may well undergo further transformations in the future.

The need for counselling is stated in several different ways: Craft develops a penetrating analysis of the background of political ideology, of economic and social structure against which must be seen the growing demand that the country's abilities should be guided and utilised for the good of the individual, as well as of society. It was this same line of reasoning in a very similar situation which led American administrators to favour the introduction of counselling in American schools in the 'fifties. Since Craft's starting point is the requirements of the state he has to confront the dilemma that faces any potential 'talent scout' of having at times to weigh in the balance the prior claims of the economy and of the individual client. The present writer, in his paper, adds to the economic reason for counselling the need for counselling the individual on a personal plane for the sake of his personal fulfilment and happiness rather than of his social usefulness.

The relations of counselling to the economy of the nation, on the one hand, and to the economics of education on the other, are themes that form a stimulating contrast in the papers of Craft and Gawthorpe. Whilst the economy in its growing complexity demands counselling for the better utilisation of talent, the cost of it would seem, according to Gawthorpe's paper, to be almost too great a burden for the economics of the schools. The larger good, one would have thought here, must be the end which will govern the means and justify the cost.

The whole area of the counsellor's relationships with the world around him forms a pattern of themes woven through several papers. Let us take the counsellor's relations with his clients—and their parents—first of all. This may often be of a peculiar intimacy which requires a special sensitivity and skill to handle. The fear of 'invasion of privacy' has, understandably, arisen in this context in the United States (cf. quotation from Cicourel and Kitsuse, p. 23). The public line against such interference will be drawn even more rigorously in this country, though the scarcity of counsellors will by itself ensure that the danger is not a very acute one. However, the fear serves to underline the desirability of both a high degree of selection and of training for counsellors, for these factors are certain to be the real safeguards against over-enthusiastic and what amounts to unprofessional action.

The second most important part of the counsellor's world are teachers and headteachers. It is precisely the fact that they are colleagues which creates the expectation and necessity of colleague-like frankness and which, as one paper suggests, might create difficulties. Gawthorpe wonders whether English headteachers would be ready to allow things to go on in their school of which they are not fully aware. Rowe's and Helen Whale's papers, on the other hand, show that headteachers *can* view this whole question as the natural expression of the counsellor's fundamental regard for the pupil's integrity (an essential attitude relevant also, of course, to the question of unwarranted probing).

The last important part of the counsellor's world are the agencies situated outside the school, relations with which will considerably affect his work. They are seeing the rise of a new profession which will make a contribution to and strengthen the existing facilities in areas with which they are concerned. The voices of two of these existing services are heard in Robb's and Catherine's Avent's papers and it is clear from them that, indeed, a new contribution is needed. If these two writers are at all representative of their professions, relations with the helping agencies will not be marred by a jealous guarding of prescriptive territories, but, on the contrary, each will try to enlist the counsellor as a helper, if not as an outpost, of its own service. This may create problems of over-demand that will have to be resolved on an empirical basis. Reading the two chapters in succession makes one realise what a remarkable collection of skills and aptitudes we require of the counsellor, what a conglomeration of duties we impose on him. In fact, one might conclude that it would take an almost superhuman counsellor to encompass them all effectively.

This last realisation is, indeed, the starting point for the final theme of the symposium: the evolution of the counsellor's distinctive rôle which surely must take place, as it does with any living organism. We may start with the 'trinity' of counselling, but we shall develop from there.

The issues that preoccupied the conference in its various discussions can, it seems to me, be divided into *pseudo-issues*, and *crucial* ones. The questions firstly of the confidentiality of the interviews and secondly whether counsellors should also teach for part of their time aroused considerable debate during the conference. Yet the confidentiality of the interview appears to me to be a pseudo-issue, because in practice counsellees voluntarily agree to the disclosure of 99 per cent. of the interview material to teachers or headteachers concerned with them and indeed have mostly already informed them of these matters. On the other hand, teachers are usually willing to respect the inviolability of the counselling interview for the 1 per cent of material for which the counsellee expects it. The teaching function of counsellors seems to me at least partly to be a pseudo-issue in most instances, because the reality of the staffing situation *at the present time* will usually dictate a solution which will be accepted as inevitable and the question will thus be resolved on practical grounds.

However, it is interesting to note that Hargreaves (1967), who set out to combine teaching with research for which he needed an open relationship with the boys, gave up teaching the lower streams after a few weeks. He found that the boys from these streams (the 'delinquent sub-culture'), but not those from the higher streams, were deeply suspicious of him and his relation with them became friendly and frank only when he stopped teaching them.

The *crucial issues*, on the other hand, that arose out of the conference appear to be these:

1. The need for counselling. There is widespread and growing awareness of the need for more systematic and professional help with the problems of adolescence with which counselling deals. The necessity of a separate professional to exercise these functions is, however, still very much under debate.
2. Training. Again, while the need for full training is gaining wider recognition, the relative importance of personality on the one hand, or professional training on the other is an issue by no means fully resolved.
3. Employment. The universities' output of trained counsellors is not sufficient by a long way to meet the needs of the schools

once the extent of these needs has been fully recognised. But meanwhile local education authorities will have to decide how many posts they are able (or feel they ought) to make available for trained counsellors.

4. Career structure. Is counselling going to be a career that the most fitted and the most able will find it worthwhile to pursue? The career structure of counselling—assuming that we shall have counsellors—is also an issue that still hangs in the balance.

The first two of these issues can hardly be resolved by administrative action. They can only be explored and their resolution advanced by further discussions, meetings, and above all, experience. In a sense further movement on these issues is basic to the resolution of the last two. Yet a move here, particularly on the third point, could also, by providing closer acquaintance with the reality of counselling and its demands and possibilities, help to advance public discussion on the questions of the need for counsellors and of training.

Action on the third issue could well take the form of an experimental scheme in which some large comprehensive school employs a number of fully trained counsellors at a specified counsellor:pupil ratio—a scheme which could, by means of systematic evaluation, demonstrate the extent of the usefulness and achievements of counselling. Such an experiment, properly set up and rigorously controlled, could be initiated by one local education authority, supported by the Schools Council. In addition, many other local authority areas could well take steps to test the usefulness of this kind of work by more informal trials in which they would deliberately fill certain of their 'counselling' or 'pastoral care' posts with fully trained counsellors. We should thus, on an empirical basis, come to grips with the basic questions at issue.

The conference and this symposium will have served a purpose if they have explored, however fumblingly, the shape and nature of a concept of counselling that fits the needs of British society and of the British educational system.

Bibliography

ANDERSON, C. A. (1967), *The Social Context of Educational Planning*, U.N.E.S.C.O.: Internat. Instit. for Educ. Planning.

ARBUCKLE, D. S. (ed.), (1967a), *Counseling and Psychotherapy: an Overview*, McGraw-Hill.

ARBUCKLE, D. S. (1967b), 'Counselor, Social Worker, Psychologist: Let's "Ecumenicalize" ' in Saltzman, G. A. and Peters, H. T. (eds.), *Pupil Personnel Services*, Peacock Publishers, Inc.

BANKS, O. (1968), *The Sociology of Education*, Batsford.

BEEBY, C. E. (1967), *Planning and the Educational Administrator*, U.N.E.S.C.O.: Internat. Instit. for Educ. Planning.

BERNBAUM, G. (1967), *Social Change and the Schools 1918–1944*, Routledge & Kegan Paul.

BERNSTEIN, B. (1965), 'A Socio-Linguistic Approach to Social Learning', in *Penguin Survey of the Social Sciences*, pp. 144–68, Penguin Books.

BLAUG, M. and WOODHALL, M. (1968), 'Productivity Trends in British Secondary Education, 1950–53', *Sociology of Education*, *41*, no. 1.

BOWDEN, Lord (1968), Social Sciences Research Council, Newsletter No. 2, Feb. 1968.

CAMPBELL, F. (1968), 'More and More Exams', *New Society*, 20 June 1968.

CARTWRIGHT, R. D. (1968), 'Psychotherapeutic Processes', *Ann. Rev Psychol.*, Vol. 19.

CENTRAL ADVISORY COUNCIL FOR EDUCATION (ENGLAND):
(1954), *Early Leaving*, H.M.S.O.
(1959) *15 to 18* ('Crowther Report'), H.M.S.O.
(1963), *Half our Future* ('Newsom Report'), H.M.S.O.
(1967), *Children and their Primary Schools* ('Plowden Report.'), H.M.S.O.

CENTRAL STATISTICAL OFFICE (1967), *Annual Abstract of Statistics*, H.M.S.O.

CLARK, B. R. (1962), *Educating the Expert Society*, San Francisco: Chandler.

CICOUREL, A. V. and KITSUSE, J. I. (1963), *The Educational Decision-Makers*, New York: Bobbs-Merrill.

COMMITTEE ON HIGHER EDUCATION (1963), *Higher Education* ('Robbins Report'), H.M.S.O.

COMMITTEE ON LOCAL AUTHORITY AND ALLIED PERSONAL SERVICES (1968), *Report*, H.M.S.O., Cmd. 3703 ('Seebohm Report').

CONANT, J. B. (1967), *The Comprehensive High School*, New York: McGraw-Hill.

CORWIN, R. G. (1965), *A Sociology of Education*, New York: Appleton-Century-Crofts.

COUNCIL FOR SCIENTIFIC POLICY (1968), *Enquiry into the Flow of Candidates in Science and Technology into Higher Education* ('Dainton Report'), H.M.S.O.

COWIE, J., COWIE, V. and SLATER, E. (1968), *Delinquency in Girls*, London: Heinemann.

COWIE, J. and KAHN, J. (1968), *Brit. Med. J. 1*, 748–9.

DAVIES, B. D. and GIBSON, A. (1967), *The Social Education of the Adolescent*, U.L.P.

DAWS, P. P. (1967), 'What Will the Counsellor Do?', *Educational Research*, *9*, 83–92.

DAWS, P. P. (1968), *A Good Start in Life*, C.R.A.C.

DEPARTMENT OF EDUCATION AND SCIENCE (1960), *Secondary School Examinations other than G.C.E.* ('Beloe Report'), H.M.S.O.

DOUGLAS, J. W. B. (1964), *The Home and the School*, MacGibbon & Kee.

DRUCKER, P. F. (1959), *Landmarks of Tomorrow*, New York: James Heineman.

HALSEY, A. H. (ed.), (1961), *Ability and Educational Opportunity*, Paris: O.E.C.D.

HARBISON, F. (1967), *Educational Planning and Human Resource Development*, U.N.E.S.C.O.: Internat. Instit. for Educ. Planning.

HARGREAVES, D. H. (1967), *Social Relations in a Secondary School*, Routledge & Kegan Paul.

HOLLIS, F. (1964), *Casework: A Psychological Therapy*, New York: Random House.

LYTTON, H. (1968), *School Counselling and Counsellor Education in the United States*, N.F.E.R.

MARSH, D. C. (1965), *The Changing Social Structure of England and Wales, 1871–1961*, Routledge & Kegan Paul.

MAYS, J. B. (1962), *Education and the Urban Child*, Liverpool University Press.

MCGEE, R. (1967), 'Education and Social Change' in HANSEN, D. A. and GERSTL, J. E. (eds.), *On Education: Sociological Perspectives*, John Wiley.

MUSGRAVE, P. W. (1965), *The Sociology of Education*, Methuen.

OHLSEN, M. E. (1964), *Guidance Services in the Modern School*, New York: Harcourt, Brace & World.

PATTERSON, C. H. (1964), 'Counseling: Self-clarification and the Helping Relationship' in BORROW, H. (ed.), *Man in a World at Work*, Houghton Mifflin.

POIGNANT, R. (1967), *The Relation of Educational Plans to Economic and Social Planning*, U.N.E.S.C.O.: Internat. Instit. for Educ. Planning.

REUCHLIN, M. (1964), *Pupil Guidance: Facts and Problems*, Strasbourg: Council of Europe.

SCHOFIELD, W. (1964), *Psychotherapy: the Purchase of Friendship*, Englewood Cliffs, N.J.: Prentice-Hall.

SCHOOLS COUNCIL (1967), *Counselling in Schools*, H.M.S.O. Working Paper No. 15.

SEEBOHM, F. (1968), See 'Committee on Local Authority and Allied Personal Social Services'.

SIRJAMAKI, J. (1967), 'Education as a Social Institituon' in HANSEN, D. A. and GERSTL, J. E. (eds.), *On Education: Sociological Perspectives*, John Wiley.

TAYLOR, W. (1967), 'Secondary Reorganisation and the Transition from School to Work' in *Aspects of Education*, No. 5, Hull University Institute of Education.

TAYLOR, W. (1968), *Half a Million Teachers*, Bristol University Institute of Education.

TROW, M. (1963), 'The Collegiate Explosion' in *New Society*, 7 Nov. 1963.

TYLER, L. E. (1961), *The Work of the Counselor*, New York: Appleton-Century-Crofts.

UNIVERSITIES' CONFERENCE (1968), *Universities and Productivity*, A.U.T.

VAIZEY, J. and SHEEHAN, J. (1968), *Resources for Education*, Allen & Unwin.

WATSON, W. (1964), 'Social Mobility and Social Class in Industrial Communities' in GLUCKMAN, M. (ed.), *Closed Systems and Open Minds*, Oliver & Boyd.

WEINBERG, I. (1967), *The English Public Schools*, New York: Atherton Press.

WISEMAN, S. (1964), *Education and Environment*, Manchester University Press.

WOODY, R. H. (1968), 'British behavioural counselling', *Ed. Res. 10*, 207–12.

Index

Achievement motivation, 19
Adaptability, 16
Anderson, C. A., 21 n.
Arbuckle, D. S., 83, 88, 90
Attlee, C. R., 10
Avent, C., 63, 75, 106
Avondale Project, 82

Banks, O. L., 16
Beeby, C. E., 21
Bernbaum, G., 20 n.
Bernstein, B. B., 11
Blaug, M. and Woodhall, M., 13
Bowden, Lord, 79
Boyle, Sir E., 26
Bureaucratisation of schools, 82

Campbell, F., 17 n.
Cartwright, R. D., 84
Central Advisory Council for Education (England), 11, 13 (see also names of individual Reports)
Child Guidance Clinic, 42, 46, 53–62, 71–4, 89, 99, 103
Children's Department, 42, 58, 89, 99
Cicourel, A. V. and Kitsuse, J. I., 15, 19, 23 n., 106
Clark, B. R., 20
Comprehensive schools, 12, 14, 24–5, 30, 37, 54, 63, 104, 108
Conant, J. B., 63, 80
Confidentiality, 30, 40, 46, 61, 99–100, 107
'Continuity of concern', 15, 37
Corwin, R. G., 21
Cowie, J., 71
Craft, M., 9, 80, 105
'Crisis counselling', 40, 42
'Crisis' in American education, 15, 81
Crowther Report, 11, 20
Curriculum
    in United States schools, 64, 80
    reform, 12, 13
    structure of, 24, 64

Dainton Report, 20 n.
Davies, B. D. and Gibson, A., 16
Daws, P. P., 12, 15, 37, 55, 57
Definitions of ability, 14
D.E.S., 17 n.
Douglas, J. W. B., 11, 12
Drucker, P. F., 20

Early Leaving Report, 11
Economy
    and guidance and counselling, 13, 81
    and technological society, 16, 25
    changing demand for skill, 17, 20
    expenditure on education, 17, 18
    primary, secondary, tertiary sectors, 16, 17
    relationship of education with, 14, 15–19
Edge Hill College of Education, 36 n., 43
Education Welfare Officers, 31, 42
'Educational priority areas', 11, 15, 19, 40, 73, 89
Egalitarian political ideology, 10–13, 22, 81
'Eleven-plus' examination, 12, 13
Examinations, growth of, 17
Extended family, decline of, 44

Fulton Committee, 29, 83

Gawthorpe, R., 29, 105
Gill, C. J., 57, 96
'Globality of concern', 12, 37
Gross national product (see Economy)

Halsey, A. H., 11, 21
Harbison, F., 18 n.
Hargreaves, D. H., 12, 107
Headteachers
    increasing responsibilities of, 12, 30
    relationships with counsellors, 30, 35, 48, 50, 100, 106, 107
Hollis, F., 88

Home-visiting, 39, 46, 50, 56, 68, 98
Housemaster system, 30, 38, 44, 50, 97
Hoxter, H., 104

Individualism (see State)
Interprofessional Research Commission, 90

Kline, P., 48

Labour-force (see Economy, Technological society)
'Life-chance', 11
Lytton, H., 10, 61, 79, 93, 103

Marsh, D. C., 16 n., 17 n.
Mays, J. B., 11
McGee, R., 18
Mental health and education, 48–9, 81
Musgrave, P. W., 16

National Association for Mental Health, 104
Neill, A. S., 25
Neuro-pharmacology, 71
Newsom Report, 11
'Non-directive' counselling, 10, 19, 61, 70, 101
Non-judgmental approach, 84

Ohlsen, M. E., 14

Patterson, C. H., 87
Pedley, R., 24
'Planned procrastination', 64
Plowden Report, 11
Poignant, R., 17, 18, 20, 21
Post-war economic crises, 13
Probation Service, 42, 46, 58, 89
Public schools, 12, 24

Reid, R. L., 93
Reuchlin, M., 11
Robb, G., 53, 72, 106
Robbins Report, 11, 13, 18, 20
Rodger, A., 64
Rogers, C., 101
Rowe, A. W., 35, 106

Schofield, W., 71
School Care Committee, 46
School health service, 41

School Psychological Service, 49, 54, 57, 62, 98, 99
School records, 40, 100
School social workers, 11, 82, 89–90
Schools Council Working Paper No. 15, 10
Seebohm Committee, 91
Sex education, 46, 82
Sirjamaki, J., 18
State, relationship of individual with, 19–23
Staying on at school, trend towards, 11
Streaming, 11, 40

Taylor, W., 13, 14, 16 n., 17, 23
Teacher-pupil ratio, 32
Teacher/social workers, 11
Teachers, 17–18, 24
Technological society
  adaptability of labour force, 16
  social mobility, 74
  structure of economy, 16, 22
Training of counsellors, 34, 36, 43, 50, 53, 66, 82–5, 99, 107
Tyler, L., 14, 80, 84

Underdeveloped countries, 18
Underwood Report, 54
Universities' Conference 1968, 13

Vaizey, J. and Sheehan, J., 17

Waste of talent, 13, 21
Watson, W., 16 n.
Weinberg, I., 12
Welfare state, 10
Whale, H., 44, 106
Wiseman, S., 19
Woody, R. H., 61, 101
Working class
  adolescents' interests and outlook, 12
  and careers guidance, 67, 68
  and extended education, 42
  need for educational guidance, 11
  participation in selective secondary education, 11, 13, 24 (see also 'Educational priority areas')

Youth Employment Officers
  And use of aptitude tests, 55
  co-operation with schools, 9
  relationship with counsellors, 46, 63–70, 74–6, 99